"Trust those who search for the truth,
be skeptical of those who claim to have found it."

THE OPPOSITE OF NAMASTE
BY TIMBER HAWKEYE

EACH CHAPTER IS
A TRANSCRIPT OF AN EPISODE
FROM THE BUDDHIST BOOT CAMP PODCAST

FOR MORE INFORMATION,
PLEASE VISIT BUDDHISTBOOTCAMP.COM

HAWKEYE PUBLISHERS
Los Angeles, California

Library of Congress Control Number: 2022943921

Food for Thought

The chapters in this book are short and easy to understand,
and can be read in any order.

If you enjoy this book, please share it with your friends.

Sign up to receive one email from Timber each month
at BuddhistBootCamp.com/email

Join our online community on
Facebook and **Instagram**
@BuddhistBootCamp

Subscribe for free to the
Buddhist Boot Camp Podcast
wherever you listen to your podcasts.

This book is dedicated to you.

The Opposite of Namaste

One definition of "Namaste" is "The divine within me acknowledges the divine within you." It's a reminder that divinity resides in each of us, and the greeting helps us regard everyone as holy.

This is easy to do when we are surrounded by loving, generous, and considerate people who treat us and others with kindness and compassion. But, what happens when you come across someone who is rude, hostile, impatient, or greedy? It becomes difficult to see them as divine, which is why I think we need a term for the opposite of "Namaste;" something that says "The ego in me acknowledges the ego in you." After all, I've been rude, hostile, impatient and greedy before (haven't we all?). So, "The opposite of Namaste" immediately makes everyone more relatable, and it stops us from falling into the trap of thinking ourselves superior to anyone.

Everyone does what they do because they believe it's a path to happiness (or they wouldn't do it). And people won't stop doing what they do if they still find value in it. That's all there is to it.

Personally, I have either knowingly or mindlessly purchased clothes or electronics that were made through slave labor, and I have eaten food that tasted good even though its production was harmful to the environment and to other beings on the planet. I am no saint. Once I knew better, I started doing better, but not a moment before.

From the perspective of radical self-awareness, whenever someone acts out of their ego, I totally get it (there's an ego within me, too), so there is no judgment whatsoever. "The opposite of Namaste" removes any and all belittling of others because we wouldn't see them as any different from us.

"The ego in me sees the ego in you."

People will continue doing "bad" things, but that wouldn't make us any better than them. Let's not to criticize what we haven't even made the effort to understand, for once we understand, there is nothing left to criticize. We have all experienced how powerful and blinding the ego can be.

When you complain about somebody else's behavior (whether you personally know them or not), it's because you jump straight to judgment without making the effort to understand them. So, next time you are upset with someone, remember that we all have an ego within us that can overpower the divine. The ego's main obsession is self-preservation at all costs. It is not concerned with healing or altruism; it is solely fixated on making itself happy.

With "The Opposite of Namaste" in mind, can't you already better understand more people in your life? Maybe you can even see yourself more clearly?

Having said all that, I am NOT suggesting we come up with an actual word to say aloud to anyone (this mantra is to only be used in your head). Just look at everyone and think to yourself: the ego in me acknowledges the ego in you, and the divine within me loves the whole of you (ego and all).

This may just be the skill we need to level the playing field. It will certainly do away with any "holier than thou" attitudes.

Non-Judgment Day is Here; your participation is encouraged.

> "Next time you walk into a room full of people,
> instead of trying to impress everyone,
> find something impressive
> about everyone you meet."

Am I Normal?

The dictionary defines the word "normal" as "conforming to what is typical, usual, or expected." Some people choose to conform to social standards, and that's what makes them "normal." I just wish I had looked up the definition of the word earlier in life because I thought "normal" was how we all start out (except for some people who miss the mark, and by "some people," I mean me).

From a young age, I was told something was wrong with me because all I wanted to do was stay in my room to read or draw in silent solitude. I spent hours building model airplanes out of tiny parts, and learning computer programming code when PCs were first introduced. I wasn't into any of the typical stuff that a parent would expect from a young boy: I was quiet; I didn't like getting dirty; and I was (and still am) extremely sensitive to noise. I needed things to be very orderly to remain calm, and my violent outbursts were the result of being forced to do what was unnatural for me. I just couldn't relate to the other kids in school, and even when I did make friends, my parents ridiculed them for being as atypical as me.

My mother used to physically force me out of the house because she wanted me to play with the other children in the neighborhood like a "normal kid." I remember my dad arriving home from work one evening and finding me sitting outside on the steps. "What are you doing out here?" He asked. "Mom locked me out of the house again," I cried.

My parents just wanted what they thought would be best for me (a life with less ridicule and more "fitting in.") They had no idea what to do with a little boy who was totally unlike his older sister, a social butterfly who was always out with her friends.

When I was about to start high school, I was thrilled that my parents decided to move us to the United States. I figured I could reinvent myself, and none of the kids with whom I grew up would be around to make fun of me. Unfortunately, being a foreigner who didn't speak any English, coupled with all the other ways I was already far from typical, only meant it didn't take long for kids in my new school to make fun of me as well. Sadly, I resorted to doing whatever it took to fit in as "normal" in order to win the approval of my peers. But the harder I tried to mask and fit in, the more inauthentic and unhappy I felt.

I was 13 years old when we moved, which is when a boy turns into a man (at least according to Jewish tradition), so I was on a mission to figure out what it even means to "be a man." To the guys at school, "being a man" meant that I needed to get laid as soon and as frequently as possible, so I did. I lost my virginity at 13, but I'm not proud of it. I started sleeping around a lot, but I did it for all the wrong reasons. It screwed me up for a long time, and for the next decade, I associated sex with self-worth. I slept with anyone who wanted to sleep with me, I wore whatever clothes were trendy at the time, and I spent hours memorizing lyrics because I thought knowing the words to pop songs would make me popular (it didn't).

Later in life, to fit in with whatever was perceived as "successful," I set out to make a lot of money, so I took a job that I absolutely hated. I now wonder if we try to "find ourselves" through the years, or if we actually already know who we are, but since the world tells us to "fit in," we basically audition for different roles until we nail one that gets us a standing ovation, and that's the role we commit to playing. I moved to a new city every five years, and reinvented myself like a stand-up comedian trying out new material on different audiences to see what works.

After a few years, I went back to the drawing board to get in touch with the real me. When I reconnected with an old girlfriend, she said she had always visualized me as a caged hawk that needed to fly, yet spent his life behind bars. She was so happy to see that I had spread my wings. "It's wonderful to see you so free," she said. The figure with huge wings on the cover of my memoir, *Faithfully Religionless*, represents liberation from the past, from convention, affiliation, and association. I'm just me.

My parents' disapproval of me had nothing to do with me. They had written a script for my life before I was even born (a role for me to play), and they even decided what kind of person I should become, the kind of job I should have, whom I should marry, and what I should believe.

Over the years, they tried using guilt and shame to manipulate me into cooperating with their vision. And when that stopped working, their hearts broke.

The life my parents still want for me has nothing to do with me. They are disappointed because THEIR dreams haven't come true, instead of being triumphant that MY dreams have.

A wise woman once told me that when you walk to the ledge of the platform, you are full of excitement; when you stand on the ledge, you are full of fear; when you jump, you are full of joy. But if you never jump, you live with regret. So, whether you are 17 or 75, spread yours wings regardless of what people might say.

I am not normal (by definition). And since pretending is considered "normal," as is deceiving, saving face, avoiding confrontation, and playing life's game by somebody else's rules, I don't WANT to be normal. It's like a shoe that doesn't fit.

I'm not surprised many of us spend years of our lives thinking there is something wrong with us. Attempting to be someone we are not creates so much pressure that we either end up having a breakdown or a breakthrough. One usually leads to the other.

After years of being called weird, strange, odd, and insensitive—all negative terms that suggested I was different from others in bad and undesirable ways, I learned I am simply Neurodivergent, which finally explained how and why my mind processes data and feelings in ways that Neurotypicals don't always understand, let alone accept.

5

While most labels like "normal" are damaging, restricting, confining, segregating, and compartmentalizing people into structured identities and denominations, limiting what we can and cannot be, Neurodivergence is expansive rather than marginalizing, most akin to a breath of fresh air.

Allow me to explain that this is not a disorder, it's an operating system that works just fine. Sometimes, however, communication can break down. A friend actually snapped at me once, "You are so random, Timber! We were talking about French Fries, and you're asking me about speed boats! How are the two even connected?!"

So, I told him, "French Fries are made out of potatoes. Idaho grows more potatoes than any other state in America. A few years ago, I learned how to water ski on a lake in Idaho with my friend's speed boat, so I was wondering if you knew anyone with a boat."

To him, my thinking process made no sense, but I don't understand how anyone thinks about anything without going through this progression. I can't drink water without thinking about its entire cycle from rain to rivers, pipes, filters, all the way to the glass in front of me. Most notably challenging, aside from being very literal, my brain can't process conflicting data (like when people say they care about their health yet drink alcohol). My mind gets stuck in a loop, thinking, "It's one or the other, you can't do both." Or when someone says they love me but then treats me in ways that aren't loving, which is it?

And without making anyone too uncomfortable, I see dogs, cats, rabbits, chickens, and cows in the same light, so it doesn't make sense to put one on a plate while petting the other. When my thoughts cycle through contradicting information like that in a loop, it's like a computer program that's about to crash. It's very unsettling and disturbing, so life becomes a challenging obstacle course through various situations (such as overstimulating environments, conflicting data, loud noise, etc.), all of which can cause a crash.

Imagine asking someone for chips and they give you French Fries. As soon as you realize they are British (and French Fries are called Chips in the U.K.), nobody is "weird," "wrong," or "stupid." Nothing negative is implied by Neurodivergence any more than someone being British; it simply means we see and understand the world through another lens. So, let's expand our vocabulary to accommodate a raised awareness. Let's stop using negative words like "weirdo" or "freak," and start getting curious about the many paths up this mountain of life, not just the trail most traveled.

I once saw a coffee mug with a saying on it that read "Success means being happy." It blew my mind. In all the years I'd heard about success from my parents, teachers, employers, and society at large, "success" always involved a lot of money, a big house, a fancy car, and a family with kids, but nobody ever mentioned happiness!

Don't get me wrong, you probably can be happy with those things, but you can also be miserable with them and happy without.

I may not be successful according to society's definition of success, but I am happier than anyone I know, so according to me (and at least one old coffee mug), I am, in fact, successful.

To me, authenticity is imperative for true happiness. Don't attempt to be normal by trading in your authenticity for approval.

Be you.

The world will adjust.

> "Authenticity is the daily practice
> of letting go of who we think
> we're supposed to be,
> and embracing who we are."
> — Brené Brown

Don't Worry, Be Mindful

We worry about our appearance, deadlines, quicksand, shark attacks, killer spiders, and muggings. It makes me think of the quote by Mark Twain: "I have lived through some terrible things in my life; some of them actually happened."

While I don't know if we can ever completely stop worrying, we can learn to let go of our worries as soon as they come up. Mindfulness is not only the gap between impulse and action, it can also be a gap between thoughts. When you worry that you may have forgotten to lock the door when you left the house, that thought doesn't need to spiral to concern that you will be robbed of all your belongings and the insurance company will deny your claim because there was no sign of a break in; or that you will end up bankrupt, homeless, and alone. One thought does not need to start an avalanche.

We've grown so uncomfortable with the unknown that we worry about worst-case scenarios. We spend so much time and energy entertaining delusions until we have no energy with which to enjoy the present moment. We basically rob ourselves of our own joy. When our mind is focused on anything but the present moment, we run the risk of getting stuck in the past or worrying about the future. And when we believe negative thoughts as if they were real, we actually feed our unreasonable fears and growing anxiety.

Even if you meditate for only five minutes a day, the benefit will impact other parts of your life. For example, when you start having negative thoughts, you catch yourself the way you do during meditation, and bring your awareness back to the present moment. It's like a steering wheel for your state of mind.

I could have said, "Don't Worry, Be Happy," but then you'd ask, "How?" Well, I think we do it by choosing where to focus our thoughts. As Carlos Castaneda said, "We can make ourselves happy or miserable; the amount of work is the same."

Feelings

Since I am not a visual artist, I will try to paint with words how I relate to feelings.

Imagine yourself as a bottle of sparkling water. All the various feelings that are possible for you to experience are the bubbles inside. Some feelings stay at the bottom for a very long time before they rise; others are close to the surface; and a few quickly float to the top and disappear. The bubbles certainly make life interesting, and without them, our lives would be flat and dull. Fascinating as they may be, it's best not to get attached to any of the bubbles, nor to hope that some of the bubbles will last a long time, or to pray that others will never surface. Feelings show up and disappear without much warning. Reacting to every bubble can be exhausting, but keeping them bottled up is also dangerous, because if we get agitated, we explode. So, what do we do with all of these feelings?

I've been taught to observe feelings as they come up without identifying with them. In other words, witness the feelings without claiming them as your own. You know how there is often a voice inside your head telling you one thing, while another voice says something else? Well, you are neither one of those two voices. You are the one hearing them argue. The same is true with feelings: you are not the bubbles, you are the one observing them come and go.

In *Buddhist Boot Camp*, I wrote about the difference between feelings and emotions. If we get attached to a temporary feeling, it becomes an emotion that can last a lifetime (which is how some people stay angry for decades). Emotions, in other words, are the long-lasting narratives we create around temporary feelings.

All feelings are either painful, pleasurable, or neutral. Imagine a triangle where one point is pain, the other is pleasure, and the third is neutrality (which we can also call ignorance).

When I feel neutral about something, it's usually because I don't know enough about it (the ignorant point of the triangle). The more I learn about it, the less neutral I feel about it, and the more prone I am to either enjoy it (the pleasure point of the triangle), or dislike it (the painful point).

When I feel neutral about someone, it's usually because I don't know enough them (the ignorant point of the triangle). The more I learn about them, the less neutral I feel about them, and the more prone I am to either like them (pleasure), or dislike them (painful).

The middle of the triangle is a safe space called Serenity, where we are not neutral, nor do we harbor any strong feelings for or against anything. Serenity is synonymous with peace, clarity, and tranquility; and the opposite of serenity is turmoil and unrest. We don't spend much time in serenity (the middle of the triangle) because we are too busy seeking pleasure or avoiding pain.

Serenity may not sound appealing to you if you actually enjoy drama and chaos. It's possible you even thrive when oscillating between being extremely passionate about things or fiercely against them. Many people live their entire lives that way, never resting in serenity. All forms of media intentionally dramatize the information we process, offering us written, audio, and video stimulation around the clock to spark reaction. But just because the emotional rollercoaster runs 24 hours a day, it doesn't mean we have to ride it (especially when riding it distracts us from slowing down to enjoy serenity).

We can only see things clearly when we are serene. The rest of the time, our perception is colored by feelings that distort reality. In the center of the triangle, we know that feelings are not facts. It's a place where we can peacefully observe the bubbles appear and disappear.

Life can be peaceful if we choose to spend more time in the middle of the triangle, and less time bouncing between extremes. The choice is ours to make depending on the kind of life we want to lead. What do you choose? And why?

Not Knowing

When we sit down to watch a movie or read a book, we don't want anyone to spoil it for us by telling us how it ends. We love the unexpected twists in the plot and enjoy a surprise ending, which is why we watch live sports instead of simply checking the final score. The thrill comes from not knowing what will happen next.

At the same time, however, we are obsessed with wanting to know what the future holds. From parents wanting to know the gender of their unborn babies, to asking them as early as five years later, "What do you want to be when you grow up?" Strangers ask, "Where do you see yourself ten years from now?" And some people even pay fortune-tellers for a glimpse into the future.

Most of our anguish stems from our discomfort with uncertainty. Organized religions attempt to ease that discomfort by telling us exactly where we came from and where we are going. Eastern philosophies try to ease our discomfort by acknowledging that while we can't know where we are from or where we are going, rest assured that you will be okay no matter what. Both paths demand predictability from an arbitrary world.

Mindfulness, on the other hand, invites us to embrace uncertainty and celebrate not knowing what comes next, how the movie is going to end, or who will win the game. Is it possible that nirvana is simply the letting go of the need to know?

Although the path of mindfulness makes sense, it goes against the narrative around which we have constructed our lives with schedules, written contracts, savings and retirement accounts, promise rings, investments, and other plans for a future that may never come.

Having grown up in a war-torn part of the world, we never knew when the next bus was going to be blown up or if we would one day finally wake up to peace in the Middle East; both felt imminent. And in romantic relationships, when your partner says, "We need to talk," they may propose marriage or tell you they are leaving; nothing is certain. In fact, them leaving could turn out to be the best turning point of your life, or maybe marriage ends up being the dream-come-true; nobody knows because knowledge is an illusion. The day we admit that we never truly know anything is perhaps our day of liberation from anguish. Sometimes, what didn't work out for you, really works out for you.

In order to practice letting go of my personal need to know, I've been doing a little experiment with my meditation timer. It is set to ring a bell one time at the start of each meditation session, and three times when the session is over. The timer has presets for a three-minute session, five minutes, 10, 15, 30 minutes, or an hour. Until recently, I selected the duration for my meditation and then sat down for that predetermined length of time. Now, I click on one of the preset timers with my eyes closed. The bell chimes once to begin the meditation, and I have no idea if it will chime again in three minutes or in an hour. I just keep my eyes closed until it does. It was uncomfortable at first, but now I find it exciting!

To further practice letting go of the need to know, I read books without even glancing at the back cover; I watch movies without first seeing their trailers; I say goodbye to the people I love as if we will never see each other again (which makes seeing them again the following week all the more exciting, if it happens); and I consider every day a blessing so that I don't take any for granted.

This experiment has transformed my life in many positive ways. It eliminates expectations, enriches relationships, deepens my practice, and amplifies my sense of gratitude. I remind myself that the only thing I know for certain is that I don't know anything for certain. I'm learning to love not knowing when the meditation bell will chime, how long relationships will last, or when I'm going to die.

So, even if you somehow know what the future holds, don't tell me. I don't want to know.

Personal Boundaries

Whether we do it consciously or not, we regularly enter into agreements with the people in our lives. We decide what's acceptable, what's out-of-bounds, and what's open for discussion. These boundaries become the rules of the game by which we play.

I'm not sure if the laws have changed since I was a paralegal in the nineties, but if you were a landlord with a tenant who signed a rental agreement to pay you $1,000/month, but then you accepted a check from them for only $500 because they couldn't come up with the full amount, the law said that the moment you cashed the $500 check, you effectively voided the written contract and entered into a new verbal agreement in which the new rent is only $500. When landlords tried to take their tenants to court for back pay, the judge always said, "If anything less than a thousand was unacceptable, why did you accept five hundred?"

Most of the questions I get are from people who have a difficult time setting boundaries. The first problem presents itself when people think setting boundaries means controlling someone else's behavior, but the rules are your own to designate and yours to honor. When I set personal boundaries, I do it to control my own well-being by limiting my exposure to what I consider harmful. My motivation is self-love and preservation, not control or manipulation.

If I choose not to be around smoke or alcohol, for example, I'm not telling other people what to do, I'm choosing a healthy environment for myself. One person may be happily married to someone who drinks a glass of wine with dinner every night, but I wouldn't go on a single date with a drinker; that is my personal boundary based on what I consider harmful. And that's the second challenge we come across: people's definition of "harmful" tends to oscillate between extremes. On the one hand, some consider anything that is mildly annoying or slightly uncomfortable as "harmful," which makes them intolerant of almost everyone and everything. If that sounds like you, consider the possibility that the problem isn't other people but rather your short fuse. On the other extreme, however, some people don't think anything short of physical abuse is harmful. It's important to never assume any two people have the same threshold of what's off-limits, out of bounds, or unacceptable. We decide and convey what's acceptable when we choose to accept it.

When it comes to setting boundaries, think about what it is they are designed to protect. Imagine there are two "beings" within you: the Ego within, and the Divinity within. Our precious little Egos demand respect from others and thrive on people's approval, while the Divine already has plenty of self-respect that doesn't rely on anything external to feel validated. When we have self-love, nothing can harm us, so there is nothing we need to safeguard. The next time you feel defensive, ask yourself, "What am I protecting?"

In the smallest nutshell possible, confronting people who upset us instead of confronting our egos is like blaming the rain for soaking us instead of using an umbrella.

When talking about boundaries, think of them as agreements or contracts you impose upon yourself (not restrictions you put on others). Keep in mind, however, that if you don't communicate your personal boundaries with others, and then they cross a line, it's not their fault for not knowing where the line was drawn. Can you imagine a rental agreement without a set payment amount, or any sport without a designated field? Boundaries are essential.

Ultimately, what we put up with is what we end up with.

I'm not victim-blaming. I'm intent on each of us acknowledging our self-worth and the value of our time, energy, inner peace, and having a safe space. Define your boundaries and stick to them. If the rent is a thousand a month and you accept less, you're effectively saying that less is acceptable.

Define what "harmful" means to you, and you will be one step closer to setting healthy boundaries.

Distractions

When you decide to embark on a path of self-improvement (be it a new diet, a relationship, a book to read, a plan to get out of debt, exercise, or meditate), despite your best intentions, distractions keep pulling your attention toward something more stimulating. The challenge isn't necessarily choosing which path to take, it's staying on your chosen path without taking every exit to see what's there.

Even if we make a conscious decision to focus on something, it takes actual strength to say "No" to anything that isn't that. However, in the same way we are able to develop muscular strength through exercise, we can develop mental strength through mindfulness practice. Without this practice, the mind tends to wander off. Have you ever read one page in a book, then glanced at your phone to read a text message, then craved something sweet, so you grabbed a treat, and then two pages after you got back to reading, you wanted something salty, and then got thirsty? Suddenly, you have forgotten what the chapter is all about, so you give up on reading and check your social media feed instead. One post leads to another, and you get lost in stimulation. What happened to the goal you had, the intention you set, and the vision you want to manifest?

Distraction is destruction of all our dreams and aspirations.

So, we decide to get serious. We turn off the radio, TV, and phone. We find a quiet corner in the house to sit down, and just when we think we have safely escaped interruptions, internal distractions rush in one by one. It's no surprise; we have trained our minds to seek stimulation, so when there is no music playing over the loudspeakers, songs just plays in our heads.

There is, however, another part of our mind similar to that quiet corner in the house. It's a sanctuary where we don't try to get rid of distractions, we simply choose not to react to them. Like the weeds in my backyard; I know they are there, but I'm not pulling them today. I know there is a new message in my inbox, but I'm not going to check it right now. Something my friend said earlier bothered me, but I'm not going to be bothered by it until later (if at all). The key is not to try to stop unwanted thoughts, the key is to redirect them.

The Buddha taught the way to overcome our difficulty concentrating is by getting absorbed in something else. When Tyler Durden from *Fight Club* was talking about enlightenment, he said, "It's not a weekend retreat. You decide your own level of involvement."

In a world that condones multitasking, let's practice single-tasking (instead of switching between tasks, stick with something until it's either done, or, at the very least, extending the duration of our concentration). Begin to pay attention to what you pay attention to. You'll create new patterns until you can read a book from beginning to end without glancing at your phone, for example. This will not only benefit your meditation, you will also get better at concentrating in other areas of your life. It's a gift that keeps on giving.

Focusing on just one activity at a time enriches our experience, deepens our communication, and increases the quality of our productivity. The sooner we notice our mind drifting away from the task at hand and bring it back, the less likely it will try to escape again. Get to know how your mind works, stay one step ahead of it, and you will be better able to stay on your chosen path. That ability to focus has enough power to reduce distractions from our minds until we can close our eyes in the middle of Times Square during rush hour and be transported to an empty field in the country without a care in the world.

In the same way you create an area in your home for meditation, imagine a room in your mind to which you can go, close the door, flip the "Do Not Disturb" sign, and stay there for a few minutes. It may be uncomfortable at first, but it will become your favorite place.

Inside of you there is a sanctuary to which you can retreat at any time. The more often you visit it, the easier it will be for you to find.

Accountability

We've been learning about accountability since childhood. To get good grades in school, we had to study; to get paid, we need to work; and if we want clean clothes, we must do the laundry. It sounds straightforward, but there is a growing trend defying that logic, where people not only believe they deserve privileges they haven't earned, but no matter how much they get, they still believe the world owes them more. Psychologists can't explain this sense of entitlement, but Buddhism refers to those afflicted by greed, jealousy, obsession, and compulsion as Hungry Ghosts with huge appetites that can never be satiated.

Mindfulness highlights our accountability for our own inner peace. We can't live a positive life with a negative attitude, just like we can't expect to have food in the fridge if we didn't shop for groceries. In high school, when I thought my boss wasn't paying me enough at my first job, I felt entitled to all the office supplies I stole, convincing myself I had earned it all through my hard work. At the first law firm that hired me, we represented landlords evicting tenants who didn't pay their rent yet felt entitled to stay. I have seen people show up late at the airport and get mad at the airline for taking off without them. And we have all been (or witnessed) drivers expecting traffic on the road to part like the Red Sea. As the joke goes, "Everyone faster than me is crazy, and everyone slower than me is a jerk."

Society's growing sense of entitlement is prevalent in many areas of our culture, but let's discuss something that most of us have experienced: road rage. At one time or another, we have all been on the giving or receiving end of it. I got my driver's license on the day of my 16th birthday and immediately started delivering pizzas in San Francisco. For almost three decades so far, I've driven in almost all fifty states across America, and in various countries around the globe. In third-world countries, roads are often shared by cars, mopeds, bicycles, tricycles, cattle, buses, goats—you name it. It sounds chaotic, but there is very little road rage. If someone wants to go faster than the vehicle or livestock in front of them, they don't demonize the slow-moving traffic, they simply drive around them with no animosity whatsoever. They might toot their horn as a courtesy to let the other person know that they are in their blind spot, but it's not done out of anger or spite. It's just a friendly way to say, "Hey, I'm about to pass you. Don't be alarmed."

Recently, however, I was a passenger in a car driving on the freeway in Southern California, where the culture is VERY different. We were cruising along in what Americans call "the fast lane" (the lane on the left in the U.S.), while vehicles driving slower than the posted speed limit are urged to keep to the right. I was in the back seat of the car, and the driver was driving slightly faster than the maximum speed allowed by law. Unfortunately, as is often the case in this country, the driver in the car behind us suddenly started flashing his high beam lights and honking the horn for us to get out of his way. Yes, you read that right, HIS way.

This is a touchy subject for many drivers, so I want to be clear: I am not talking about country roads where tractors slowly drive halfway on the shoulder so others can pass, nor am I talking about certain states in the U.S. where the left lane on two-lane roads is reserved strictly for passing. I'm talking about multi-lane highways where the speed limit is largely ignored, and nobody is going fast enough for anybody else (even when they are driving the maximum speed allowed by law). If the Buddha were alive today, he might change the name from Hungry Ghosts to Speed Demons, but the affliction is the same.

To lighten things up a bit before I keep going, this reminds me of the joke where a police officer pulls someone over for speeding, and the driver asks the cop, "Do you know who my father is?" To which the cop responds, "Why? Did your mother not tell you?"

If accountability feels like an attack to someone, they are not yet ready to acknowledge their own behavior. So, if that sounds like you, then you might want to skip the rest of this chapter (for now).

After all, this is not about speed limits or other drivers, it's about whatever is brewing underneath the rage and animosity we have toward others. This is about the entitlement, the greed, the self-centeredness, and our general preoccupation with our own desires at the expense of others.

If we understand that when you want clean plates, you do the dishes, it logically follows that if you want to go faster than the driver in front of you, go around them. It doesn't matter who you think is right or wrong. If you have the expectation that the world should run according to you, THAT is the source of your misery—not the other drivers, not your landlord, and not the airline.

If what you really want is to be happy (truly happy), without any internal or external conflict, then align your beliefs, words, and actions. It's the only way to be happy, and nobody else can do it for you. Trying anything else is like trying to cut water.

We cannot be at war with ourselves and live at peace at the same time; it's just not possible. The Buddha understood this, and psychologists agree.

This is not a personal attack on you; I promise. I just want us to be mature enough to admit that Hungry Ghosts are never satisfied. It's nobody else's responsibility to make you feel good about yourself. We each have our path, and nobody can walk it for us.

Many crave validation and to have their sense of worth at least recognized if not celebrated by everyone else. But at the risk of sounding insensitive, that's the textbook definition of a codependent relationship, except it's with the entire world.

Accountability is empowering.

> "Work out your own salvation."
> — The Buddha

Fear

Imagine a heavy bag of dirt on the floor. It's in the middle of the path between your front door and the bathroom, and you have to walk around it or step over it multiple times a day. It's an obstacle at which you frequently curse, regularly trip over, and sometimes stub your toe against. All that chaos, yet you refuse to clear the path because it would require too much work, it's just "too heavy;" or the excuse I hear most often: "That's easier said than done."

People regularly choose to live with the dirt and bruised ankles rather than do whatever it takes to clear their path. Walking around the dirt **seems** easier because it involves no heavy lifting, but passivity is a behavior pattern that contributes to our own suffering. Before we know it, that pattern presents in other areas of our lives as well.

Depending on childhood household dynamics, many of us took our very first steps on eggshells, so we may not be aware that life without landmines is even an option. If we don't clear our path as adults, life can quickly turn into an obstacle course, especially when we end up with multiple piles of dirt to navigate around.

We are not talking about actual dirt, eggshells, or landmines, of course; we are talking about real world obstacles, such as miserable jobs that we refuse to quit, toxic relationships we can't seem to abandon, dietary or fitness indecisions that affect our health, uncomfortable living situations from which we could move but don't, and so on. All too often, making big changes seems like too much work, so we keep on keeping on.

Is this phenomenon a simple case of not trusting ourselves, or are we the human equivalent of the terrible urban legend about the frog-in-hot-water (where a frog will immediately jump out of boiling water to save itself, but if the water is very gradually heated, the frog will remain in the pot until it boils to death)?

What are we waiting for?

Growth is uncomfortable, but so is staying in situations you have outgrown. Are we waiting for someone to save us? Why don't we rescue ourselves? Do we feel undeserving of a better life? Are we looking for permission to change? I ask because my well-educated, intelligent friend just told me she needs to get her therapist's approval before taking the first step to ending her unhealthy marriage.

Indecision is a decision in-and-of-itself. People tell me that even getting fired, though initially tragic, ended up being the best thing that ever happened to them. I've heard countless personal accounts of people moving to a new city, state, or country (scary as it was), kickstarting a wonderful new life. These success stories are not rare… tragedy is. What will it take for us to trust our ability to thrive?

When I say our behavior patterns present themselves in different ways (the way we do one thing is the way we do all things), imagine there are certain topics you are uncomfortable discussing with anyone (even your spouse, doctor, or best friend). You are more likely to spend your life avoiding those conversations than you are to invest time to overcome the discomfort itself. That's exactly like walking around the dirt on the floor instead of cleaning it up; it's fear holding you back from fully living. A fear of heights, for example, would have you looking at the Eiffel Tower from the ground instead of seeing Paris from the top. Fear will run your life if you let it.

I am terrified of public speaking, yet I am able to do it multiple times a month because I am less afraid of fear than I used to be. The shift is in seeing fear itself as a speed-bump, not a dead-end. Once you do that, you realize that even 100 piles of dirt can be removed with some diligence, determination, and patience (it's why we work on building those skills in the first place, isn't it?)

Go slowly, of course, but go forward. When you love yourself, you make better decisions (and the reverse is also true).

We are not just products of our past; our decisions today affect our tomorrows. So, start now.

Decision Fatigue

Every decision we make throughout the day renders our next decision more difficult to make. It's called Decision Fatigue.

When you go to a restaurant, it's easier to decide what to order from a menu with three options than it is from a menu with fifty. The same is true for someone with a closet full of clothes. They might say they don't have anything to wear, not because it's true, but because having too many options can be overwhelming.

I'm a big fan of making certain decisions that minimize choices in the future. I shave my head once a week, for example, so I never need to look in the mirror or worry about the wind, hair products, or haircuts (I'm saving time, I'm saving money, and I'm saving myself from Decision Fatigue). I'm never torn about buying or keeping anything I don't actively use (I remind myself that if I don't own it, then I don't have to dust it). My breakfast is the same every day (nutritious, enjoyable, and easy to prepare). And I have five identical gray T-shirts, two pairs of pants, and all my socks are the same. These decisions were made to simplify my life and help me live the minimalistic lifestyle that I personally enjoy a lot more than I'd ever enjoyed fixing and worrying about my hair or picking out an outfit.

And since the way we handle the small decisions can influence the way we approach the bigger questions in life, this line of thinking can be applied to our core values. If you decide to always be honest the way I've decided to wear gray, for example, then you'll never be conflicted about lying again. You wouldn't ask yourself, "Should I tell them the truth? Should I not?" Because the decision to make truth one of your core values had already been made. Same can be done with the decision to be kind, generous, calm, and patient.

By simplifying our lives this way, we can reduce Decision Fatigue and avoid internal conflict. This helps us stay on the path toward being the kind of person we wish to be.

Pray Well with Others

I recall an article about a guy who got in trouble at a bookstore for moving all the bibles into the Fiction section. Between different denominations, various cults, countless sects, numerous schools of thought, and as many philosophies as people in the world, it's difficult to know what to believe, who to follow, and how to separate truth from fiction.

In California, there is a church located across the street from a Jewish temple. Once a month, the rabbi delivers the sermon to the Christian fellowship, and the minister addresses the synagogue. The important message is that although they are across the street from one another and represent different religions, they are not enemies.

There is a lot of confusion about Buddhism because it has over 800 different schools (some in direct conflict with one another, and a few that even contradict the Buddha's teachings). Buddhism is not based on belief, it is based on rational experiment. In other words, Buddhism is something you do, not something you believe in. It's more of a philosophy than anything resembling religion, especially since it has no God or creation theory. Having said that, you may come across people who insist that Buddhism **is** a religion (and even refers to Siddhartha as "Lord Buddha.") But Siddhartha (the Buddha), was not a god. He never claimed to be a god, the son of God, or even a messenger of God. He was a flawed human like the rest of us, who simply gained clear perspective of the world through nothing more than human effort. Buddhists do not worship false idols (the statues merely serve as visual representations and reminders that we can wake up to our interconnectedness and interdependence). Buddhism is a practice different from religious dogma; it's more like the practice of yoga, from which everyone can benefit regardless of what they believe. The same way we can stretch to become more flexible, we can each meditate to awaken from our illusion of separateness.

Buddhism is not in conflict with organized religion. The practice doesn't challenge the existence of God, it simply uses the word Emptiness as a placeholder for what religions call God, and what spirituality refers to as Energy (or the Universe, Spirit, Brahman, or Higher Self).

Without heaven or hell in Buddhism, everything is simply the result of consequences (action and a subsequent reaction, a cause and effect). There is no Satan on whom to blame everything negative in the world, only the awareness of darkness within each of us that can drive us towards greed, hatred, and ignorance. Luckily, we can overcome the darkness by reflecting the light in the world. It's our responsibility to save ourselves and others through compassion and kindness. The origin story of Buddhism is not only secondary, I might go as far as to say it is completely irrelevant for the practice itself (certainly not important enough to argue about).

As I've heard the Dalai Lama say at a retreat, "Do not try to use what you learn from Buddhism to be a Buddhist, use it to be a better whatever you already are." (i.e. be Christ-like rather than Christian).

There is no such thing as a "bad Buddhist" because there are no commandments to follow, just invitations for each of us to contemplate. If the teachings resonate with you, great! But if they don't, simply leave them for now.

When someone asks me if I'm a Buddhist, I don't quite know how to answer. I am a lot of things, and not one of them defines me. The important thing is that my practice doesn't keep me from being able to pray well with others.

> "When mindfulness is present,
> the Buddha and the Holy Spirit are also there."
> — Thich Nhat Hanh

Balance

People often say they are trying to find balance in their lives (whether it's balance between work and play, between excitement and relaxation, or between companionship and solitude). But a healthy balance is not something we "find" like loose change between the couch cushions. Balance is something we need to consciously create, adjust, and maintain on a regular basis. We understand this concept when it comes to balancing our checkbooks or having a balanced diet, both of which require mindful diligence.

A common question I get is, "How do I balance a slow, spiritual life with this fast-paced and technology-driven world?" The key is controlling the technology in your life instead of letting it control you. It requires new habits, discipline, and creative time management, but it's do-able.

Since we are the ones responsible for the imbalances in our lives, we are the ones who are also responsible for adjusting the scales. We can do that by turning off our cell phones at night, for example, not responding to work-related emails when we are not at the office, limiting ourselves to one hour of social media each day, and so on. The list of suggested boundaries is not only endless, it varies greatly depending on your digital drug of choice.

A few years ago, I saw a bumper sticker that read, "If you are not outraged, then you are not paying attention." Does that mean we need to stop paying attention if we want to remain calm?

Initially, that's exactly what I thought, which is why I blocked all of my exposure to media for many years. But I don't think we need to completely unplug from television, our phones, or the Internet. What we DO need to do is safeguard ourselves from getting swept away, submerged, and finally drowned in the constant ocean of information that we consume with our eyes, ears, or energy.

So, where do we draw the line? How much television is too much television? How little news is too little news?

The answer has less to do with quantity and more to do with adjusting the negativity to which we are exposed to balance with some positivity as well.

The same way we filter harmful germs out of our drinking water, we need to install a filter in our lives to limit our consumption of harmful information from the media. I believe we CAN pay attention without being outraged because rage has never improved any situation, it only makes things worse.

I've been taught that everything I am currently angry about is stopping me from being happy. And, when I decide to let go of my anger, I find that happiness was patiently waiting for me to rediscover it all along.

There is no need to react to everything we see, hear, or read. Certain things in the world will continue to upset us, at which point we can make decisions in line with our values, but we don't need to do it with anger. Compassion is an equally good motivator without the negative side effects. That's what balance looks like.

As I often say,

"Promote what you love
instead of bashing what you hate.
Tell me what you stand for,
not what you're against."

What Motivates Your Actions?

Mindfulness is the gap between impulse and response.

Mindful speech is when we pause before speaking, and make sure that what we are about to say is **true, necessary, and kind.** If the words are in line with our values and they actually need to be said (response versus reaction), and we are truly the ones who need to say them aloud, then we find a way to speak kindly or not at all. Finally, we look for the intention behind our proposed action to be certain it isn't ego-driven.

Each month, I host discussion circles at various locations throughout California. One time, while on my way to discuss this very topic of intention, I needed to stop and refuel the car. The station was packed with multiple vehicles backed-up behind one another. One pump was out of order, and when it was finally my turn, I noticed the driver at the pump next to mine was not filling up his tank. He was just sitting in his car, talking on the phone. With such a long line of cars waiting behind him, I was tempted to tap on his window and motion for him to move out of the way. But I stopped myself.

Yes, what I wanted to say to him was true, necessary, and kind, but when I asked myself if what I wanted to say needed to be said by ME, that was a show-stopper! I am not the station attendant, but... wait a minute, an attendant WAS inside the store. I actually thought about going in there to tell the attendant what was going on outside so that HE could do something about it. But, then I laughed at myself again, realizing I was still trying to control the situation (this time by thinking about telling the attendant how to do his job). Oy!

Regardless of how good-hearted my intention to help all those drivers in line may have been, I still have no definitive answer as to what course of action would have been best (if any). So, I just filled up as quickly as I could and got out of the way.

After all, I had no idea with whom the driver was talking on the phone or what was going on in his life. I didn't know if he was oblivious of the situation, intentionally rude, or simply numb at the end of what could have been a tragic day for him. Also, there was no way to know how this driver would have reacted to me had I said something. He could have apologized and moved out of the way, or he could have pulled out a gun.

We can't ever know what other people are thinking, or why they are the way they are. What we CAN do is question our own intentions, and in this case, mine was all about control. My ego's sneaky little sidekick wanted to shine, make itself known, and perhaps even be the hero who saved the day.

As we talked about this scenario in our discussion circle later that night, I discovered another reason that stopped me from turning into the traffic police earlier in the day: embarrassing as it was to admit to myself (let alone to a room full of people), I have been that guy before! I have parked my car at a fuel pump and gone inside to use the station's restroom, for example, or to buy a bag of pretzels with no consideration of the space I was taking up.

I still don't know if doing nothing about the situation at the station was cowardly or skillful. If nothing else, I have vowed to never again do what he did; and maybe that's the big takeaway.

Mindfulness is about making time to scan our actions to uncover the motivation behind them. If we don't like what we see going on internally, we can change accordingly.

When we talk about change, it's not about telling the person in the other car what to do, it's about getting to know ourselves and our own intentions.

> "Be mindful of intention.
> Intention is the seed that creates our future."
> — Jack Kornfield

Priorities

My friend Julie and her husband argue about the "right" way to do laundry. He loads the washing machine with dirty clothes, adds a cup of detergent on top, turns on the machine, and walks away. Julie, on the other hand, is a firm believer in starting the water flow, pouring-in the soap, and then adding the dirty clothes to the mix. They both want the same result: clean clothes.

It reminds me of working in the kitchen at the monastery, where two members of the staff were asked to peel and cut 10 pounds of carrots into small matchstick-sized strips. It took them four hours, which drove the efficiency expert in me crazy. I asked the head of the kitchen why they didn't just use the food processor (which would have completed the task in minutes). He explained to me that the goal wasn't to get the job done as quickly as possible, it was to offer the students four hours of mindfulness practice in the kitchen.

I failed to contemplate the WHY behind his instructions. The food processor would have chopped those carrots in minutes, that's true, but the kitchen manager prioritized the meditative mindfulness practice over efficiency and expediency (at a Buddhist monastery; go figure!). Why do we assume we know what's best? I went to the meditation hall and sat with my ego until it agreed to play nice.

We excel at judging what people do and how they do it, but we fail miserably at trying to understand the WHY behind their actions. When we share a similar goal with someone, yet their priorities differ from our own, their actions seem backward to us, counter-intuitive, silly, and even "wrong."

My friend Sheila and her wife both want to "Make America Great," but Sheila thinks we will get there by closing the borders to all foreigners, while her wife believes immigrants make America great in the first place.

We each want what we individually think is best, but what we think is best is determined by our priorities. The question we need to contemplate is, "What is the WHY behind people's actions?" Otherwise, we go through life assuming our perspective is not only right but superior.

Saint Francis of Assisi knew the importance of seeking to understand rather than to be understood.

We cannot wrap our heads around other people's logic by using our own. But when we get curious about people's ultimate intentions, and we contemplate the WHY behind our own actions, we often find a lot in common with everyone around us (even with the people with whom we couldn't previously relate).

The real question becomes whether your priority is to truly understand the person in front of you, or to prove yourself "right" by making them "wrong?"

If you keep getting irritated by someone who refuses to change, it means you are also refusing to change.

Inner peace is the first step we can take to live in peace with others, so let's vow to take that step together.

> "The one who asks a question
> is a fool for five minutes.
> The one who doesn't ask,
> remains a fool forever."
> — Chinese Proverb

Life As an Experiment

I treat everything in my life as an experiment, which gives me flexibility to not be attached to an end result or a goal. I go into every situation thinking, "Let's try this for a while and see how this experiment works."

Some of these experiments have lasted a few months, and some have continued for 10 years. It's important to re-evaluate as we go along and frequently question things that made sense a decade ago, a year ago, or a month ago, and ask "Does it still make sense today?"

We tend to think our choices about who to date or where to live are huge, monumental decisions that are going to completely redefine our lives. Each course of action steers us in a new direction, but almost every option (short of the decision to have kids), can be reversed, and we can make a new decision the very next day.

Right now, for example, we can decide to wake up in a new city tomorrow morning, or create a new life with a different job and new friends. We have so much power when we let go of fear (which is what normally holds us back from making a decision that seems "permanent" when, in fact, nothing is permanent).

At one point in my life, I moved from San Francisco, California, to Seattle, Washington. Seattle is still my favorite city in the world, but after years of living there, I one day decided that I wanted to play beach volleyball every day of the year (not just during the one month of summer the Pacific Northwest sometimes gets), so Seattle was no longer conducive to the new kind of life I wanted to lead. That's when I moved to Hawaii, which was great for ten years, until life took another turn, this time rendering Hawaii no longer conducive to the new life I wanted to lead.

Imagine how difficult it would have been for me to move if I was clinging to California, Washington, or Hawaii. This flexibility in one area of life tends to lend itself to everything else we do.

When I took the monastic vows, for example, I was in full robes for two years, which made sense while living in the monastery (we all had the same haircut and the same monastic robes, which visually depicted what we believed: that we are all one, all connected, with no differences among us). But when I left the monastery and wore the robes at the airport and around town, people treated me as if I was different, and I was responsible for that. The same robes that communicated "we are all the same" in the monastery, screamed, "Look at me! I'm different," when worn outside of those walls.

My ability to let go of the robes was only possible because I wasn't attached to them. They were an experiment until it no longer made sense. I still follow the vows, but I no longer wear the robes.

We can apply this perspective to relationships, jobs, dietary restrictions, and so on. Try something for a while, and if it works, great! If you find out later that it doesn't work, great! It's a sign that it's time to move on.

Treating everything as an experiment in our own lives also makes us more understanding and compassionate when someone else does something that we think is a bad idea. We can take a step back and think, "They are just conducting an experiment, and they will do it until it doesn't work."

Our job, as friends, is to love the people in our lives through their own experiments and to be supportive.

Experiment with that.

> "Remember that Failure is an event, not a person."
> — Zig Ziglar

Intention

When my friend realized he was spending more than six hours a day on his phone, mostly scrolling through social media apps, he changed the homescreen on his phone to display the message, "What is the best use of your time?" Now, when he grabs his phone, nine times out of ten, he puts it right back down and does something else. His one intention now is to make the best use of his time, all the time, and it has improved every aspect of his life (home-cooked meals replaced drive-through restaurants, exercise replaced adult websites, and books replaced TV shows).

Setting a single intention behind everything we do is a great way to stay balanced. The alternative is to have the intention behind your job be to simply make money, for example, a different intention motivating your dinner plans (to suppress those hunger pains), another intention behind buying clothes (perhaps to keep up with the latest fashion trend), and a whole other intention behind watching TV (as a form of escape or numbing). It would be like wearing one mask at work, another at church, a third behind the wheel, and so on... it would be exhausting!

What if you have **one** overriding intention, and it's to always pick the healthiest option in front of you regardless of what you do (when you shop, watch TV, or sit at the dinner table); would your choices be different than the ones you are currently making?

If we always buy the most expensive things in order to impress other people, we might go bankrupt because the intention itself was detrimental to our well-being. Conversely, if we always buy the cheapest option, we might forego our well-being for the sake of a few pennies. That's why we need to be mindful of the intention already behind everything we do (even when we're not always consciously aware of what it is). Without mindfulness, motivations like fear, greed, and desire end up running/ruining our lives.

Around the time I took the monastic vows, I set one intention as the motivation for all my actions: it was (and still is) to awaken, enlighten, enrich, and inspire a simple and uncomplicated life, and to offer food-for-thought so we can all live at peace with the world (both within and around us). Regardless of where I'm invited to speak (bookstores, churches, corporate retreats, or maximum-security prisons), I never do it for money or fame; I do it with that specific intention in mind. In addition to keeping me grounded, focused, and purposeful (as in full of purpose), it also stops me from doing what isn't congruent with my values.

If my repeated invitation for us to live in line with our values sounds like a daunting task, perhaps this proposal to set a single intention is a way to simplify the process. I want to be clear, however, that it's not enough to simply set the intention, we need to follow through with it and act accordingly. As Oscar Wilde said, "The smallest act of kindness is worth more than the grandest intention."

Keep in mind that intention and impact do not always align. We can only control our intention and our actions, but we have no control over how our actions are perceived or received by others. This is a good opportunity to practice letting go of outcome, focus on the journey, do the best we can, and take nothing personally.

If this all sounds like a hybrid of Toltec, Christian, psychology, and Buddhist teachings, that's because it is. Let's take the wisdom a step beyond inspiration and actually implement it in our lives.

Why wait until we die to rest in peace? Let's set the intention to be peaceful while we are still alive!

If we were to meet today, instead of asking what you do for a living, I would ask, "What is your intention?"

What would your answer be?

My Panic Attack

After six years of accumulating airline mileage points, I finally had enough to cover a free round-trip flight and five-week backpacking trip around the Philippines.

Setting up a tent on the beach (or as I like to call it, a five-billion-star hotel), made it a nature lover's paradise, but also made it necessary for me to get quite a few shots and vaccinations for things like typhoid and malaria.

I took the malaria pills for two weeks prior to departure, every Monday during the trip, and for three weeks afterwards. I didn't bother reading the possible side effects because not taking the pills wasn't an option, but it didn't take long to notice the pills made me sleepy, for example, so I took them at night. I later discovered they also cause vivid dreams and a slight fever, but that wasn't a big deal.

The point of the trip was to maximize time on quiet, deserted islands for peace and tranquility (and to avoid major, loud cities like Manila as much as possible).

I have always been hypersensitive to certain sounds (Misophonia makes the high pitch of CRT monitors unbearable for me, and the same goes for beeping alarms, someone snoring or chewing, the auditory assault of emergency sirens, wind chimes, screaming children, and even certain bird calls). Avoiding noise isn't an option when dealing with major airports and public transportation. The noise would drive me crazy if it weren't for two things: I can usually meditate and breathe deeply to remain calm until the silence returns, and I almost always carry earplugs in my pocket just in case the sound is louder than my meditation can soothe.

During this five-week vacation, I experienced wonderfully warm ocean breezes on white-sand beaches, lots of hikes, a beautiful sunrise trek up one of the highest peaks in the country, clear blue skies, and great food.

It would be dishonest of me not to mention the trip also involved one incident of getting lost, two bouts of seasickness, and three cases of food poisoning (which I think came from drinking the water, not necessarily from anything I ate). It was still a great trip in the grand scheme of things.

After a couple of weeks of reading books in a hammock on a quiet deserted beach, I returned to the loud and busy city of Manila to catch a flight to a neighboring island. The sudden noise of construction, traffic, car horns, blaring TVs and radios, along with the fast-pace of everything and everyone around me, shot my anxiety through the roof, and sent me into the worst panic attack I've ever had.

I am not going to downplay the experience for you; I truly believed it was the end of the Timber we know. I figured the *Buddhist Boot Camp Podcast* would cease operations, and I would need to check myself into a mental hospital upon returning to the States (if I didn't kill myself first). That's how bad it felt! Suicide was more inviting than another minute of the noise from which I couldn't escape.

I didn't recognize myself. I mean, I'm typically the guy who can meditate and breathe deeply through most discomfort, but nothing was working.

What got me through the sudden spiral of mental instability was repeating the following three words to myself over and over again: this is temporary, this is temporary, this is temporary.

Within an hour, I fell asleep (it's incredible how much energy the body uses to feel something—anything—so strongly).

When I woke up the next day, I was no longer on edge, but I still seriously questioned my mental health. Was this my own psychotic breakdown? It felt like the years of meditation, mindfulness, and all the practice I've had to remain calm in the midst of chaos amounted to nothing.

I later discovered that severe panic attacks are a common side effect from the malaria pills. It was a relief that this was a chemical reaction to the medicine, but it felt so real.

In the moment of panic, I couldn't access all those other parts of my brain that would have otherwise kicked in with logic and reasoning to talk myself off the ledge. What helped was the mantra "This is temporary," which carried me through to the calm shore of serenity.

"Temporary" can mean a minute or two, an hour, a month, a year, or a lifetime. No matter how we look at anything, everything is in constant flux. What surprised me the most was how quickly I was willing to accept my mental breakdown prior to falling asleep.

I wanted to share this story with you because all of the years of mindfulness practice did NOT go out the window in the moment of panic. The gap between impulse and response may have been shorter, but I still managed to remind myself how temporary it was.

On this vacation alone, mindfulness got me through hours of being seasick on the worst boat ride imaginable; it got me through the panic attack; and it got me through the whirlwind of change to which I came back when I returned home in March of 2020.

This is temporary.

> "The primary cause of unhappiness
> is never the situation itself
> but your thoughts about it."
> — Eckhart Tolle

Desire

When I initially heard the Buddhist teaching that desire is the root of suffering, I couldn't accept it without asking some questions. Isn't the desire to alleviate suffering the very motivation behind Buddhist practice? Wasn't the Buddha driven by a strong desire for deeper understanding? Doesn't desire propel us toward enlightenment?

The answer, it turns out, is both Yes and No. A desire for world peace, for example, can motivate us to continue choosing a peaceful course of action even while we understand worldwide peace is unrealistic. But, if we desire anything to such a degree that we are miserable unless we achieve it, that desire ignites and fuels our suffering. Perhaps better stated, **it's not that desire is the source of suffering, it's that true happiness is the absence of desire**.

Consider the cause of your anxiety. It stems from wanting things to be different than they are. The antidote to that desire is acceptance. But acceptance is not approval. Accepting things like war, racism, global warming, and animal cruelty, doesn't mean we stop doing what we can to minimize the harmful ripple effects of our actions; it means we accept it all as part of the current reality while we remain peaceful. Because if we don't, we become part of the problem we are trying to eradicate. When you hate the hater, you become a hater.

So, while it's true that desire is at the root of our suffering, it's not the whole truth and nothing but the truth so help us Buddha. Anytime a teaching is reduced to bite-sized quotes, we don't get the full context of its meaning. This is yet another invitation to realize that happiness is not something we need to pursue (it isn't "out there" in the distance). We simply need to remove whatever obstructs our access to happiness (e.g., fear, expectations, greed, hatred, ignorance, and yes, desire), and Voila... There it is!

When we want less, we suffer less.

Meditation Misconception

I don't meditate to control my thoughts; I meditate so my thoughts don't control me.

There is a common misconception that meditation is about clearing the mind and making it quiet. It's why many who try meditating for the first time quickly give up, exclaiming their thoughts were racing nonstop, and they couldn't turn their brains off, which is what they believed was the goal.

Even after years of meditating, my mind still wanders whether I'm in meditation or not. Now, however, when I watch my mind running around like a puppy playing in the backyard, I can call it back at any time; sort of like saying, "Come here, boy!" And the mind obeys.

It's not about tying the puppy to a tree with a short chain so it doesn't go anywhere (that would be cruel and only drive it mad and more resistant to structure); it's about differentiating between play-time and paying-attention-time. The key is balance and discipline.

If you've ever had a dog, you know that even when they are well-trained, certain things still grab their attention. If your dog sees a squirrel, he will ask with his puppy eyes, "Can I please chase it even though I know I can't catch it?" Our mind doesn't run after squirrels; it just keeps chasing thoughts with more thoughts, often in the form of worrying (which usually turns out to be a complete waste of time).

Part of mindfulness practice is the ability to decide when the mind can run free and when it needs to sit. Otherwise, it's like the dog taking YOU for a walk instead of the other way around. That metaphor might not resonate with you if you are not into puppies, so let's look at the quote, "Nobody can drive you crazy unless you give them the keys."

If we compare life to a car ride, then we need to be selective about who we allow into our car, and certainly picky about who gets to ride in the front. So, first things first: claim your spot in the driver's seat with your hands on the wheel. Random thoughts will cross your mind, and some thoughts will be as disturbing as roadkill on the shoulder of the road, but those thoughts are not you; they are byproducts of everything to which you have been exposed. Unless you seal yourself off in a bubble, unsettling ideas are bound to infect your thoughts (from violence in movies or on the news, to songs that can easily hook your attention and try to hijack your mind). The idea is not to turn off the world around you; that would be like closing your eyes while you drive.

It's funny how we try to control so much in life when most of it cannot be controlled. Some people even call themselves "control freaks," yet invest very little effort into learning how to control the one thing we can: where to focus our attention. Once we learn how to do that, we can respond instead of react to what's happening around us. To do it skillfully, we need to practice. It's no different than learning any other skill.

Meditating so your thoughts don't control you doesn't have to be done cross-legged with incense burning. You can meditate while jogging, painting, gardening, or even while brushing your teeth. The moment your mind wanders, bring it back.

Start by watching your mind like you would watch a movie. Go into "the theater" and pay attention to what's happening on the screen. Watch the movie in your mind with curiosity, not judgment. When your thoughts stray, you will see that all these thoughts are just like advertisers trying to grab your attention. You do not have to buy everything they are selling. You can just say, "Thank you for the information," and move on. It's very liberating and precisely why I don't meditate to control my thoughts, I meditate so my thoughts don't control me.

Why We Share

Without anybody asking, my friend Sophie tells everyone that she is vegan. She then proceeds to tell them how much they would benefit from changing their diet as well. According to her, she only wants to "help people see the light." Unfortunately, all they see is another crazy vegan putting jackfruit on their plate and calling it "pulled pork." When I asked her why she does this, she said, "Sharing is Caring, isn't it?" I'm not so sure it always is.

Under the pretense of "Sharing is caring," a few organized religions send missionaries door-to-door to spread the word of God, to recruit new members into their church, and to offer people another shot at salvation. The Salvation Army actually coined the term with a trademark in 1950, guiding us all to "share what we have **with those who are less fortunate**." And that, right there, is the problem.

Don't get me wrong: offering food and shelter to those who have none is great, but for anyone to view someone with different beliefs as "less fortunate" is anything BUT caring, loving, or kind. In that instance, sharing is demoralizing. It's when someone with a superiority complex thinks they are "helping" those who are "inferior" or "less fortunate" because of their views.

That superiority complex is exactly what sent me running from Judaism in the first place, where believers chant "Adonai Hu Ha'Elohim," which means "My God is THE God" (implying all other gods are false). Oy!

It's a slippery slope because here I am sharing my views with you, so how is this different? I used to think it had to do with the intention behind the sharing, but that's not it at all. I mean, Sophie has good intentions when she talks about her plant-based diet, and the missionaries seeking to save people from eternal damnation are also trying to "help." So, when does sharing stop being an act of caring and start becoming a form of harassment in disguise?

The distinction, I believe, is determined by whether we are ASKED to share. I understand why "Bible Pushers" (as they are called) shout about their faith from mountaintops after it has enriched their own lives so much; I want to do the same thing when I discover a new restaurant that blows me away. What I NEED to do, however, is practice restraint and avoid talking about it **unless** someone actually asks me if I know a great place to get something specific to eat.

My buddy Bill didn't tell anyone about his cancer diagnosis, treatment, or recovery, because he knew everyone would bombard him with their opinions of what they think he "should" or "shouldn't" do. He feared they would send him books and articles to read, drown him with information (with the best of intentions), but drown him nonetheless.

What drew me to Buddhism is its "hands off" approach, where each practitioner simply vows to be kind and do less harm, but never to recruit. Jesus can't be blamed for what is being done in His name, and if a Buddhist temple tries to recruit you, it's a business move, not a Buddhist one.

Remember: forcefully trying to lure someone to do ANYTHING (even if it's to embark on a spiritual path), is the work of the ego using guilt, shame, or fear disguised as compassion. As one of my teachers used to say, "You can't give by throwing!"

We each need to pause, contemplate WHY we share what we do, with whom, and for whose benefit?

Before speaking, or texting, or posting something online, ask yourself: was I asked? Is this necessary to say? And does it need to be said by me?

Our egos make us believe we do everything for all the "right reasons," but it's not always true.

"Only speak if it improves the silence."

Victim

I have made plenty of bad decisions in my life. Some choices damaged my own well-being, and too many decisions unintentionally hurt others in some way.

What's interesting is that I have no shame apologizing for my wrongdoings, and I'm good at promising to be more mindful in the future not to repeat the same hurtful action or inaction. But, when I make decisions that are harmful to myself, the conversation in my head is not very civil. It goes something like this:

> You're such an idiot!
> How could you be so stupid?
> What a loser!
> Okay... calm down, you'll do better next time.
> No, you won't! That's what you said last time.
> Come on, if this was a friend, you would tell them to relax.
> But this isn't a friend, it's me, and I know better!
> Idiot!
> [Repeat all of the above on a loop....]

Every time I made a mistake, that voice bullied me into believing that I was the worst human being on the planet. As if the damage from the mistake wasn't bad enough, I made it worse by beating myself up about it. This continued for years until I realized that of the many bad decisions I've made in my life, not forgiving myself was by far the worst.

For the concept of forgiveness to even exist in our social construct, we create the duality of a wrongdoer versus a victim. When we assume the role of the victim, we expect an apology so we can then play the role of the compassionate forgiver (or not). But it's all a power play.

I'm not saying we shouldn't apologize (more on that later). I'm saying the person I'm inclined to dub as the "wrongdoer" doesn't need to apologize in order for me to forgive them (they don't even need to be sorry). Forgiving is a gift you give to yourself (the entire process is internal). Receiving an apology is not a prerequisite that we need to demand, but apologizing is definitely a standard we can set for ourselves (note that saying, "I'm sorry you feel that way" is not a sincere apology). When we actually regret doing or not doing something, it's imperative that we apologize for our action, not for the result of that action.

Again: **apologize for the action, not for the result of the action.**

THAT is what taking ownership looks like. It is vulnerable, raw, perfectly human, and absolutely beautiful. It doesn't imply "I'm indebted to you until you choose to forgive me," because that essentially translates into, "Now, it's my turn to play the victim."

A sincere apology is comprised of: "I messed up (taking ownership of past actions), I am very sorry (present), and I will try my hardest not to do it again (future)."

You can even follow it up with, "Is there anything I can do right now to make things better?"

It's not the traditional "I'm sorry" and "I forgive you" model, but it removes guilt, shame, and victim mentality, and it makes space for empowerment, betterment, and progress. In this model, nobody is "indebted" to anyone else, and that applies to your past and present selves as well.

This is much healthier than the vicious loop of blaming and waiting for forgiveness from ourselves or from others.

Ask yourself if you want to stay stuck or if you want to move forward and onward.

> "We are all walking each other home."
> — Ram Dass

Namaste Indoors (Pandemic Reflections)

In 2020, most of us who weren't working in the medical, emergency, or public service sectors, stayed home to stop the spread of the Coronavirus. Some people embraced their newfound solitude as an opportunity for introspection and contemplation, while others were climbing the walls, riding their emotional rollercoasters.

We are accustomed to routines, schedules, and constant busyness, so when we were advised to "shelter in place," many of us didn't know what to do with ourselves.

It reminded me of my first day at a Japanese monastery. We were shown to our meditation cushions in the zendo; everyone sat down facing the wall; the bells chimed; and that was it. We weren't given any instructions on what to do, and there was no visible timer counting down the minutes. We just sat in silence and waited for something to happen.

At first, many of us found this idleness difficult to handle because we are typically surrounded by physical, visual, and auditory stimuli. It can be jarring when everything stops. But if you have ever meditated before, you know that stillness is where the real work begins. When we turn off the external stimuli, we can finally get in touch with what's going on internally.

After staring at the blank wall in the zendo for a few hours each day, week after week, that wall became a mirror, reflecting all the internal issues I had been ignoring or hiding since childhood. Even matters I thought I had worked through in the past resurfaced. I had no choice but to reevaluate my personal responsibility for how my life had turned out; figure out whose voice was in my head judging my every move; and finally ask myself why I do what I do. This empowered me to steer my life in an entirely new direction. I was more consciously aware of my internal voice because I had quieted everything else enough to finally hear it.

When the pandemic started, some people embraced their newfound solitude as an opportunity for introspection and contemplation, but many doubled down on the amount of news they watched to combat the silence of self-isolation. This backfired, of course, sparking panic and anxiety.

If anxiety has taught me anything over the years, it's that panic never makes anything better.

Self-isolation can go hand-in-hand with personal growth when we embrace the stillness. One word changed my attitude about sheltering-in-place: I wasn't STUCK at home, I was SAFE at home.

What we lost in the pandemic was our illusion of stability and our false sense of security and control. Mindfulness teaches us to wake up to the beauty of uncertainty and the reality of impermanence. I hope you emerged from isolation more appreciative and grateful than ever before.

Get to know yourself better so you can be refreshed, improved, and filled with gratitude.

In other words, keep calm and... that's all, just keep calm.

> "They said a mask and gloves were enough
> to go to the grocery store,
> but they lied!
> Everybody else was wearing clothes!"

Validation

At a *Buddhist Boot Camp* event, a father in the audience mentioned that his young kids need constant validation and approval. He wasn't sure where they had picked up that behavior pattern.

We discussed a parenting technique to which many of us have been subjected growing up: rewarding good behavior and punishing the bad. It seems like a logical parenting style, but as a result, we looked to our parents to validate that we are, in fact, "good," while we tried to avoid being called "bad."

As children, that's how we created the first narrative about who we are. Those of us who were called a constant disappointment to the family and told that we would never amount to anything, grew up believing exactly that until we changed the narrative. Change is not a quick fix; it often requires years of therapy, support, introspection, and contemplation.

So, if you constantly praise your children, they will grow up seeking praise from everyone around them. But, if you point out their flaws, they will believe they are flawed. Either way, the issue is validation.

If how I feel or think about myself is contingent upon someone else's opinion of me, then my sense of self-worth would fluctuate up or down depending on who I'm around—an exhausting way to go about our day.

Relying on validation from other people for our sense of self-worth puts us in a codependent relationship with the entire world.

I know that within me is the potential for greed, hatred, and ignorance, as well as the option to be selfless, kind, and compassionate. No longer depending on others for my sense of self-worth is freedom. It's up to me to maintain this serenity by aligning what I think, say, and do. Living congruently, it turns out, is more reassuring and sustainable than constantly looking for validation from others.

Look at your own values and how you live your life. If those values are not reflected in what you think, say, and do, then you have some work to do.

If nothing else, this commitment to live congruently with your own values eliminates the anguish and disappointment that come from constantly expecting other people to affirm that you are good enough, beautiful enough, or smart enough. It's a way to give yourself the gift of true happiness, not contingent on outside validation, but on your own inner goodness expressing itself outwardly.

In other words, to validate your own sense of self-worth, simply do good to feel good. It's that simple.

And if you are raising children, remember this quote by Glennon Melton: "Don't let yourself become so concerned with raising a good kid that you forget you already have one."

"Release old concepts
that keep you in self-punishment patterns.
Let go of old stories
and create from a place of love
and self-validation."
— The Buddha

Discipline and Dedication

The other day, I sat down to meditate, closed my eyes, and as soon as the timer chimed to signal the start of the 30-minute session, I wondered if I had remembered to open the window before sitting down. Although I was tempted to open my eyes to check, I kept my eyes closed until the second bell signaled the end of the meditation. It was tempting to open my eyes because I really wanted to know what was going on with the window, but why? It wouldn't have made any difference; I wouldn't have gotten off my cushion to open it mid-session anyway. The window's status in that moment was completely irrelevant. Realizing it was not relevant is what fueled my discipline and dedication to keep my eyes closed with patience, mindful breathing, and a smile on my face.

Imagine a pendulum where on one extreme we are careless about something, and on the opposite end, we are fiercely engaged. The middle ground between the two extremes is carefree, untroubled, and relaxed. This made me wonder if acknowledging things as irrelevant is the key to that ever-elusive middle point of inner peace between negligence and concern. For those thirty minutes, whether my window was open or shut was completely irrelevant. That word typically feels harsh and dismissive, but intentionally dismissing certain thoughts is the very skill we develop by focusing on what's relevant. In Buddhism, that practice is called Discernment.

In choosing a title for this chapter, I was torn between "Dedication" and "Discipline," so I decided to go with both. Dedication is a commitment to a chosen path, and Discipline is a form of mental or physical training.

We can only actively care about a certain number of issues at any given time. If we overload our minds with irrelevant information, we shut down. Car engines overheat when they are pushed beyond their limits, computers do the same when simultaneously running multiple programs, and when humans try to process too much

49

information about an overwhelming number of issues (most of which we can do nothing about), we experience what's called Compassion Fatigue.

From issues such as mass shootings in schools and global warfare, endangered rhinos, the environment, immigration, elections, and let's not forget our own health, it's no surprise we feel overwhelmed and ill-equipped to do anything about it all. But that's just it—we CAN'T do it all, nor is anyone expecting us to do it all. What we CAN do, is one thing at a time, like sitting when it's time to sit.

The Serenity Prayer invites us to accept the things we cannot change, have the courage to change the things we can, and the wisdom to know the difference. Knowing the difference might just be the key to a profoundly serene life. It's the only place from which we can make rational decisions—as opposed to irrational reactions.

The discipline and dedication it took for me to not open my eyes during my morning meditation is a tiny example of a much larger muscle group that we can strengthen through exercise. It's a "six-pack" of sorts consisting of Commitment, Dedication, Discipline, Discernment, Mindfulness, and Awareness. Imagine the possibilities if we build THOSE muscles through repetition. I was sure the only way to put my mind at ease was to open my eyes and get the information I so desperately thought I needed, but then I realized there's another way to put the mind at ease, and it's by letting go of the need to know.

Those robot vacuum cleaners that automatically move around the floor to clean up when you're not around crack me up. When they sit in the corner, seemingly doing nothing at all, they are actually doing what meditation can do for all of us: they are re-charging.

When people ask me about breaking their existing habits, I suggest starting small by exploring the habits we don't even realize we have. Raised awareness is not only the first step, it needs to be present in every step, and that requires discipline and dedication.

Do Less Harm

A woman named Anna told me she has difficulty reconciling the same Buddhist invitation with which I struggled for a very long time: to "do no harm."

Anna was raised on a farm with chickens, pigs, goats, and cows. Some of them were designated as pets, which the family never butchered nor ate, while others were strictly raised for consumption. As a young girl, she didn't understand the distinction. Now, as an adult, she has pet pigs, turkeys, and sheep, whom she never eats, yet she would have a chicken sandwich with bacon for lunch. She's been trying to make peace with the fact that she simultaneously loves animals yet eats them. She sees bacon as someTHING, but Roger, her pet pig, as someONE.

I initially thought the conflict simply resulted from a lack of commitment to one way or the other. To illustrate what I mean by commitment, let's use the example of dating multiple people at the same time, which is commonplace, harmless, and perfectly acceptable. But continuing to date multiple people after entering into a monogamous marriage would inevitably create conflict (internal and otherwise), because a promise had been made to stay committed. Applying this to Anna's discomfort with loving animals yet eating them, was a commitment missing to see ALL animals as someONE instead of someTHING?

It is technically impossible for us to "do no harm," because our very existence is only possible at the expense of other beings. We inevitably kill living organisms every time we breathe, wash our hands, consume food, and so on. Doing "no harm" is not an option. But when I changed my mantra from "do NO harm" to "do LESS harm," I began to see every action as an opportunity to ask myself, Is the harm I'm about to cause avoidable? How can I satisfy my hunger and nutritional needs while minimizing the harm I cause to myself and to others?

You might be familiar with the practice of the Three Gates regarding mindful speech. Imagine three gates in your throat with a guard at each one. The guard at the first gate stops the words you are about to speak and asks, "Is what you're about to say true?" If the words are true, then the words proceed to the second gate. The second guard asks, "Is what you're about to say necessary?" And if your intention is both true and necessary, the words proceed to the third and final gate. The final guard asks, "Is what you're about to say kind?" If what you're about to say is true, necessary, and kind, go ahead and say it aloud.

To tie this back to Anna, we can implement a similar filter for what we eat as well. Prior to eating, three guards ask, "Is what you're about to eat true to yourself and your values? Is it necessary? Is what you're about to eat kind to the planet and kind to yourself?"

When we develop self-respect, everything we consume changes (from what we eat and drink to what we watch and read).

So, for everyone out there struggling to live healthily, mindfully, and harmlessly, I suggest being gentle.

Do LESS harm.

> "Our prime purpose in this life is to help others.
> And if you can't help them,
> at least don't hurt them."
> — The Dalai Lama

The Problem with Being Goal-Oriented

The problem with being goal-oriented and future-focused is that at no given point are we ever where we want to be. There is always an underlying bigger, higher, faster, better goal just out of reach. This mentality keeps us focused on what we **don't** have (or how much farther we still have to go), rather than appreciative of the abundance in our lives and grateful for how far we've already come.

Many people have anxiety and panic attacks, habitually imagining worst-case scenarios are about to happen, constantly fearing or worrying about all the things that could go wrong. It's been said that anxiety is caused by living in the future, whereas happiness is only attainable when we remain fully present with what is directly in front of us. I regularly scan my thoughts to make sure I am neither carrying the weight of the past into the present, nor projecting some imaginary unfolding of events that may or may not turn out the way I fear or hope they would.

Instead of the phrase "proceed with caution," the words "observe," "surrender," and "accept" come to mind, so I proceed with curiosity.

This contradicts what many of us have been told: that goals signify aspiration. But it is very possible to be motivated, driven, and determined without any attachment to an end result. The distinction is where we place our focus. For example, the highlight of my volleyball-playing days had nothing to do with any tournaments or trophies won; it had everything to do with the fact that I got to play volleyball every single day for many years. If my focus was on winning, the disappointment of losing would have overshadowed the joy of getting to play in the first place. If my focus was on winning, I would have been constantly driven to compete again, and again, and again, with a hunger that could never be satisfied. There was always another team to beat, other tournaments in which to compete, and more medals to win. I would have been stuck in a vicious loop of not-enoughness.

But since the focus was on the joy of playing (not just in hindsight but in the moment), the journey itself was the destination.

It's like eating healthy and exercising for the sake of feeling good (not as an attempt to lose weight). I work out to celebrate what my body can do, not to punish myself for what I ate.

Even leading a spiritual life is for the sake of depth, not longevity. I officiate many weddings, for example, and some couples marry for the joyous benefit of companionship, while others do it out of fear with the expectation that their partner will "always be there."

By staying in the present moment, we derive more joy from everything at hand. It's what I find most beautiful about the Tibetan tradition of making complex sand mandalas that take hours or days to create, only to be destroyed when they are complete; it's a wonderful reminder to focus on the journey, not the destination.

There is an old story about a young boy who traveled across Japan to find the school of a famous martial artist. Upon arrival, the young boy asked, "How long must I study to become the best karate master in the land?"

"Ten years at least," answered the master.

"What if I study twice as hard as all the other students?" asked the young boy.

"Then it would take twice as long: 20 years," replied the master.

"Why is it that when I say I will work harder, you tell me it will take longer?"

"The answer is clear," said the master, "When one eye is fixed upon the destination, only one eye is left with which to find the way."

> "Every day is a good day,
> some are just better."

Who Am I?

A friend who recently retired told me he's having difficulty figuring out who he is without a job. He spent his entire life working and following a routine without ever developing much of a personality. He is not alone. A personality is defined as "the mental and moral qualities distinctive to an individual."

"There is nothing distinctive about me," he said, "my beliefs are not my own (they were handed to me), and I've never reached for anything in life (except for a promotion). I have tried so hard to blend in that I faded into the background."

Few people ever question what moral qualities are distinctive to them unless certain life events force them to self-reflect. My buddy Mike wrote a book entitled *Going Om* about his time in prison, where, for the first time in his life, nobody cared that he was a CEO, a husband, a father, or anything other than Inmate #60419066. All the labels with which he had previously identified were stripped from him. It took going to prison for him to realize he was already in one. He essentially freed himself while behind bars.

A woman who recently lost her only grandchild told me she has to constantly remind herself of everything else she was before she became a grandmother, or she starts feeling like she has lost everything. And a year after my buddy Jessie came out as gay, he realized his orientation is only as much a part of him as his hair color, not his personality.

"Who are we?" is a deep question, and it's important not to confuse identity with personality. According to Jewish law, I am technically Jewish (by birth), even if I never identify as such. The questions that constantly ring in my head are How am I Jewish? How am I Buddhist? What else am I, and According to whom?

When I first heard Tyler Durden say, "You are not your job, you are not how much money you have in the bank, you are not the car you drive, you are not the contents of your wallet, and you are not your f*cking khakis," I literally owned 42 pairs of khakis, drove a sports car, and worked at a law firm. I thought that's who I was, but I wasn't even close.

Identities can be restricting and confining if we identify with our job or relationship status, our health, youth, or anything that is either temporary or directly contradicts what we know in our core to be true. Gender identity is a perfect example of how personal and individual these answers must be, rather than anyone deciding for us. But again, be it gender, religion, wealth, or health, Identity is not the same as Personality. I would go as far as to say that when we set aside the identities that segregate EACH of us, we tap into the personality (the moral quality) that celebrates ALL of us.

On the one hand, we have Buddhism, which is all about awakening to our interconnectedness, but on the other hand, personality is determined by qualities distinctive to an individual. So, which is it? I picture the Buddha sitting under the Bodhi tree and realizing that we are all one.

Who we are, therefore, is collective, fluid, and interconnected. **Something doesn't need to happen to each of us for it to matter to all of us, and nothing needs to happen to all of us for it to matter to each of us.**

Our personality is developed when any concern with "me" changes to "we," and instead of asking "Who am I," we ask "Who am I in relation to everyone and everything else?"

In answer to that question, who I am is another you, and who you are is another me.

"Life is not a process of discovery, it's a process of creation.
You are not discovering who you are, but creating yourself anew.
Seek, therefore, not to find out who you are,
but to determine who you want to be."
— Neale Donald Walsch

Accepting Yourself

Caring what other people think about us is a fascinating combination of both insecurity and self-obsession. Think about it: we spend so much time thinking about ourselves (how we look, how we sound, how we come across, and how we compare). This fuels our anxiety, stress, and depression. And when we feel empty inside, we attempt to fill that void with other people's opinions of us. We do this even though their judgment reveals more about them than it does about us. The more confident we are about ourselves and the decisions we make, the less we need the approval or acceptance of others.

When I didn't know who I was (or even how to answer that question), I defaulted to believing what others thought of me.

My friend Justin was raised by a father who called him a lazy loser, and constantly yelled at him to do better (even when he was winning trophies in sports and getting all A's in school). Nothing was ever good enough for Justin's dad. Fast forward to Justin as an adult, and despite being successful, healthy, and wealthy, he still believes he will never amount to anything. Even years after his father's passing, Justin is still trying to impress the man who was never impressed by anything anyone has ever done. This pressure affects every decision he makes, and it sucks all the joy out of everything he accomplishes because, deep down, he knows nothing would ever be good enough for his father.

Imagine how light Justin would feel if he stopped listening to his dad's voice in his head. Picture Justin with his own values, defining what "enough" and "successful" mean to him, and feeling accomplished at the end of every day for the first time in his life.

We all have voices in our heads that judge and compare us to others, but it's important not to identify with those demons. We can recognize them for what they are and start writing new narratives.

In *Buddhist Boot Camp*, I wrote about how I felt fat as a teenager after my mother made a comment about my weight. I spent the next few years getting in shape with the sole purpose of becoming a stripper at some point (because I thought the only way I would ever feel attractive would be if people paid me to take my clothes off). Well, if you've already read *Buddhist Boot Camp*, then you know that even after I did become a stripper a few years later—with an eight-pack and biceps bigger than my head—the pale chunky kid still stared back at me in the mirror.

I thought that if hundreds of people told me I was hot, it would cancel out my mother's voice in my head. But it wasn't until I stopped trying to impress my mother (or anyone else) that the pendulum swung to the opposite extreme. Today, I no longer care whether others find me physically appealing.

In Buddhism, we talk about acceptance, but we need to start by accepting ourselves. The futile alternative is making our inner peace dependent upon the whims of other people (whether we look for that external validation from our parents, friends, neighbors, or even strangers on social media).

Once we accept ourselves, we can spend the rest of our lives **caring about others, instead of caring what others think about us.**

"Care what other people think,
and you will always be their prisoner."
— Lao Tzu

Self-Love

Shortly after January first, I posted the following question online: "Could you devote this year to loving yourself more?" People responded with comments like, "That would be difficult," "I can't even imagine," "What does that even mean?" "Easier said than done," or "How would I do that?"

The entire concept of self-love used to be foreign to me, but I knew it was different from self-centeredness, which is egotistical and selfish. Whenever I explore a new concept, I try to think of its opposite, and the definition by distinction becomes crystal clear: **the opposite of self-care is self-neglect.**

Many of us are conditioned to go above and beyond for those we love, so let's make sure our own name is on the list of people worthy of our best.

There's a restaurant in Seattle with the slogan "Eat Like You Give a Damn!" In other words, "Eat like you care." But care about what? Eat like you care about your health, about the planet, about animals, about local farmers... you get the idea. Eat like you care because the alternative is eating like you don't care. Self-love starts with caring.

Each of the three times my sister found out she was pregnant, she immediately stopped drinking alcohol and smoking cigarettes. The moment she gave birth, however, she started smoking and drinking again. She said she stopped when there was precious life inside of her, but she totally failed to acknowledge there is always precious life inside of her... Her own!

Self-neglect is more widespread than I realized, and it affects many aspects of our lives, not just what we consume. So, let's move beyond simply eating like we care, to living like we care! Your life is your message, which means you don't need to tell anybody what's important to you because your actions convey this information quite clearly. Do you express self-love because you see yourself as having worth and value, or do you neglect yourself because you feel worthless? Do your decisions reflect that you care or that you don't?

When studying spirituality (whether religious or secular, Eastern or Western, everything points to sanctity within each of us. Yet, I spent many years failing to treat myself as sacred (which doesn't mean "holier than thou," but exactly as holy as thou).

One of my teachers described our body as the one coat that our soul gets to wear for an entire lifetime. If you only owned one jacket, you wouldn't throw it on the ground when you got home. You would hang it, keep it clean, and take good care of it. That simple visual made me realize I was mistreating my jacket. That's when my definition of "healthy" changed to exclude anything toxic; not just food, but also TV shows, movies, books, and even some friends and family members. My bedtime changed; I started spending more time in nature; and I began making decisions that reduced the stress in my life. I can't give you a recipe for self-love because it's going to look different for each of us. But at its core, start by caring.

It helps me to visualize two beings inside of me: the god within and the ego within. So, when I eat, which one am I feeding? If I'm tempted to hold a grudge, for whose benefit am I doing it? When I get angry, which part of me decides how to respond? Is it the compassionate side that stands for peace and kindness, or the destructive side that acts out of rage?

Get to know the god within you (or the good within you, if you prefer). First, acknowledge that it's there, and then take care of it. Pretend you're pregnant with precious life inside of you if you have to, but start living like you care, eating like you care, sleeping like you care, drinking like you care, investing in your life like you care, and you will find that by loving yourself more, you will have more of yourself to give to others.

Eventually, you will see there is no distinction between yourself and others. We are all holy. We are all worthy of love and compassion.

Not Up to Me

The impact of our actions is subject to elements that are out of our control (such as unforeseen circumstances and/or other people's perceptions). We can decide on a course of action, but we need to completely let go of any attachment to a predicted outcome or expected reaction.

When I managed an online art gallery, the value of the work was ultimately determined by the collector who wanted to buy it, not by the artist (and certainly not by me). There were times when nobody wanted to buy a complex painting that took many hours of love and skilled labor to complete, yet pieces that the artist himself thought were downright juvenile sold for thousands of dollars. Does that make the art that didn't sell worthless? Not necessarily.

A few years ago, my friend got into a terrible car accident that sent her to the hospital for x-rays. That's when a cancerous tumor was discovered early enough to be removed before it spread. If it wasn't for the car accident, who knows if or when she would have discovered the tumor. So, was the car accident a blessing? Terrible? Neither? Or both?

To add one more example, when my friend suggested that I compile the emails I had sent to her over the course of eight years and publish them as a book, my initial reaction was, "Why? Who would want to read them?" And she said, "That's not for you to decide, Timber. Just publish the book, and other people will decide if they want to read it." She saw the value of *Buddhist Boot Camp* before it was a book; I just had to trust her.

This brings us to a tricky dichotomy: on the one hand, the value of the book, the car accident, and the artwork is determined by the people impacted by them, but on the other hand, none of us are worthless even if nobody sees our worth. Buddhism teaches us that we are all Buddhas even though some of us are unable to see it. Or, if you prefer, we are all God's children, even though many of us don't feel worthy of God's love. So, what do we do?

I believe we need to get out of our own way, and catch ourselves when we attempt to think and intervene on somebody else's behalf. Let's stop assuming, presuming, or deciding things for others, but rather decide for ourselves what is beautiful, important, valuable, or worthy of our attention, time, and energy.

If someone doesn't see your worth, it doesn't mean you are worthless. The mantra "Who am I to decide?" is now constantly in the forefront of my mind.

Just as someone else's nightmare could be my personal dream-come-true (and vice versa), I default to believing that everything and everyone is valuable to someone, somewhere, depending on their time, place, or circumstance. Either way, **it's not up to me!**

Isn't that liberating? Can't you just feel your shoulders relax?

This is yet another invitation for each of us to remove ourselves from the center of the Universe.

Socrates said, "The unexamined life is not worth living," so let's give life more than a passive, dismissive, or perfunctory glance, and examine it until all concepts of worthlessness disappear. If nothing else, we'll be closer to our Buddha-nature than we were before.

The end result is not up to you.

"Expectations are planned disappointments."

Drama

You may have a friend or family member who claims that drama follows them like a tattoo on their rear. But, from your vantage point, they appear to be chasing it by getting involved in other people's drama, often without invitation. Drama can look like arguing for the sake of arguing, or complaining for lack of something more intelligent to contribute.

We may be describing your friend or your own behavior, but drama is there nonetheless, and you're not sure why.

I've made the mistake of assuming everybody wants a peaceful and uncomplicated life. I'm beginning to realize there are people who either intentionally seek chaos and turmoil for reasons I don't yet understand (perhaps for entertainment value or a thrill); or it's possible we are dealing with an addiction to drama as a means to escape (just like any other drug). This would not only make sense, it would also explain why people SAY they want a peaceful life while their actions convey otherwise.

Is it possible that meddling is just another narcotic to avoid having to face our own issues, insecurities, and shortcomings by pointing out somebody else's? Maybe the "high" is the feeling of superiority at any cost? Yogananda explained it as, "Feeling tall by cutting off the heads of other men." This would explain Internet trolls, road rage, gossip, and people who are easily offended.

Does the most dramatic and loudest person in the room want peace? Do they think this is the way to get it? Or can they not see themselves? My own wake-up call was realizing that if I truly want peace, I must start by being peaceful.

Reminds me of Jackie Kashian confessing to her teacher that she had no friends in school. When the teacher asked, "Well, are you friendly?" Jackie realized that she most certainly was not, and it all made sense. Self-realization has many moments of humor like that.

Your Behavior

Your beliefs don't make you a better person, your behavior does.

Many people assume our behavior is closely tied to our beliefs, but that's not always true. Most of us believe that lying is not good, for example, yet we habitually lie to ourselves and to others. There's a gap between how we imagine ourselves to be and how we truly are.

As an experiment, write down your core values, your intentions, and a paragraph describing the kind of person you want to be. Once that's done, cross-reference it with the person you are today, and you'll see where you have work to do.

The beautiful thing about having core values as guiding principles is that they make your decisions for you. If someone offers you a job that sounds great, cross-reference the job description with your core values to determine whether the job meets your prerequisites to live in line with your intentions. If quality time with your family is the most important thing to you, then an amazing salary isn't so great if it takes you away from them.

Gandhi said, "Happiness is when what you think, what you say, and what you do, are all in harmony." When all three are in alignment, you eliminate internal conflict. Living out of alignment creates an internal battle. You then try to escape through distractions such as drugs, sex, long hours at work, dysfunctional relationships, drama, over-involvement with the news, television programs, sports... you get the idea): anything except looking at yourself in the mirror to find the contradiction and get to the root cause of the conflict.

Your values show in how you treat yourself and the people around you, what you consume, how you respond to traffic, and even where you shop. You will occasionally slip from your listed values, but there's no judgment (replacing lifelong habits takes time). Make sure to include patience as one of your core values.

Unmet Needs

According to Nonviolent Communication (NVC), we each have a set of "needs," and every feeling we experience either indicates that our needs are being met or that we have an unmet need.

In addition to sleep, water, and food, NVC lists additional possible needs, such as a need for connection, acceptance, affection, appreciation, consideration, or inclusion. We may feel a need for a sense of meaning or purpose; for clarity or stimulation; or for autonomy in the form of choice, freedom, independence, and space. The list goes on.

The other day, my friend asked me how I was feeling, and I answered, "I feel good." To which she replied, "'Good' is not a feeling, Timber. Can you tell me more?"

So, I looked at the list of feelings she had printed out and laminated, and I was able to pinpoint that I felt accomplished, relieved, calm, centered, and grateful (which, in NVC speak, meant my needs for purpose, relaxation, information, and serenity, were all met). She looked at me with that wise smile of hers and said, "Now, isn't that a better answer than just 'good'?"

This challenge helped me better communicate what I was feeling, I had a deeper understanding of what I appreciated about the day, and my friend was able to share in my experience more fully. This is a tool for a stronger connection with ourselves and with others.

When we feel joyous, it could very well be because our "need" for connection and play are being met, while feeling frustration may simply express our unmet "need" for clarity. And when we feel jealous, it's possible that we have an unmet "need" for security, safety, or honesty. Again, the list goes on.

I keep putting the word "need" in quotes for a couple of reasons: first, I'm not convinced that what NVC refers to as "needs" are not actually preferences that we have simply convinced ourselves are needs (thereby creating a void that we then try to fill). And second, no two people have the same "needs," so it's difficult for me to make a blanket statement claiming any list of needs is universal. If I were to rewrite this age-old practice, I would say that every feeling expresses an unmet preference (not a need). That feels more honest and empowering because it puts the responsibility of fulfillment on me rather than on others.

Having said that, what I **do** like about NVC is that it never assumes to know what someone else's needs or preferences may or may not be. NVC practitioners don't assume, they ask questions. If a feeling is indicative of an unmet need or preference, then understanding what that unmet need is could stop a gnawing feeling of unworthiness, stuckness, boredom, perpetual anger, and more.

When we get better at explaining ourselves rather than expressing ourselves, others will better understand us. But if we keep expecting others to simply "know what we mean," then the misunderstandings, assumptions, challenges, and finger-pointing will continue in a vicious cycle of the shame and blame game.

Imagine the shift from blaming your feelings on someone else's action to acknowledging and explaining to them that a personal need of yours wasn't met. The other person may have had no idea, especially if a strong need of yours is not even on their radar.

A relationship is all about how people relate to one another. For years I've been writing and talking about "Explaining our anger instead of expressing our anger," but let's take it a step further and explain the unmet preference behind our anger. This will bring us closer together with loving-kindness, understanding, and compassion. Call me a hopeful romantic, but I believe people want to enrich each other's lives; they just don't always know how. So, let's be proactive in helping others understand us by better understanding and explaining ourselves. Or, as my friend says, "Let's become emotionally literate."

According to Me

Sparked by the Black Lives Matter movement, I hosted an online discussion that ignited a desire to understand how we can go beyond merely educating ourselves about systemic racism and privilege, and learn to navigate talking about these issues with our family members, coworkers, and friends.

Privilege is when you think something isn't a problem just because it doesn't personally affect you. A woman named Susan offered the following example of privilege for us to consider: when she was looking for commercial space to lease so she could open a nail salon, she rented a suite on the second floor of a walk-up building with no elevator. Because of her able-bodied privilege, it never occurred to her that this would be a problem until someone made an appointment for a manicure but couldn't get to the salon because it wasn't wheelchair accessible. Susan doesn't have to be disabled to be an ally in an ongoing effort to make all buildings and commercial spaces wheelchair-accessible. **Being made aware of her privilege didn't make her defensive, it made her a better person.**

We can all benefit from taking inventory of our privilege. During the discussions, as white listeners became aware of their privilege, black participants gently explained they don't always have the time, patience, or bandwidth to educate everyone about this issue, especially since racism is not their problem to fix.

Having these conversations with family members who don't see the problem can be tricky. Giving unsolicited advice (whether we do it kindly or not) is often perceived as an attack, which only makes people respond with defensiveness. I mean, calling someone a racist is problematic because they will either deny it and respond with aggression, or they will feel justified in their beliefs, so you would only be stating the obvious to them.

The way I have found to peacefully broach the subject is to lead by example by sharing a personal story about my own prejudices. When you talk about realizing a new truth after years of believing something else, make it about yourself rather than about the person with whom you are speaking. They will not get defensive, offensive, or shut you out. Owning up to your own shortcomings comes across as an invitation for the other person to do the same. It's easier to talk to someone when they are open and vulnerable. But when we push our beliefs on someone, we literally push them away.

This opened the discussion to how many of us had emotionally charged conversations that were not very effective. We need to learn how to stay in the present moment with no attachment to the outcome of a conversation. The alternative is repeating the same behavior and expecting different results.

The online Q&A took an unexpected political turn. The person who brought it up was upset about a certain politician, calling him "Divisive, mean, and a bad role model." My only suggestion was that she add the words, "according to me," at the end of her accusations. It is our egos that turn our opinions into facts, and then we look at people with differing views as our enemies. But adding the words, "according to me," at the end of our statements keeps our egos at bay. If we don't do that, we assume that our truth must be true for everybody. If you believe in a "Universal Truth," notice how it's always conveniently your own.

"I don't believe the world is full of lies.
On the contrary,
I believe the world is full of truths."
— Faithfully Religionless

Rude

A friend recently told me that she has gotten pretty good at being kind, respectful, compassionate, understanding, and patient with strangers, colleagues, and neighbors, but with her husband, she is very quick to get angry, raise her voice, judge, belittle, and show the ugliest side of herself. The same thing happens with her siblings and kids. And she is not alone.

I have witnessed people reserving their worst behavior for the people closest to them (the ones they claim to love the most), and then act kindly and gently toward acquaintances and complete strangers. To better understand this phenomenon, I posted an online survey, asking "Why don't we strive to be as kind, understanding, or as patient as possible with the people we love? Why do they have to see the worst in us? Why is kindness so difficult?"

An overwhelming majority of the people who responded explained the reason they are nice to strangers yet short-tempered, rude, and even downright mean and nasty toward family members is because they feel comfortable and secure with those who are "forced" to put up with them no matter what.

The answer to the survey blew my mind because I tend to reserve the very best of me for the people closest to me.

I wasn't raised in a family with whom I can be rude, mean, or disrespectful. I was raised by parents I've seen cut other family members out of their lives without a second thought. Heck, they disowned me for three years during which I was dead to them because they didn't approve of who I was dating at the time.

That experience taught me that relationships (ALL relationships), are disposable, fragile, and require tending and nourishing if you want them to continue.

In a weird way, I'm surprisingly grateful for what I initially thought was dismissive dysfunction in my family, but maybe it wasn't? I mean, I learned how important it is to be nice to people you love, and to seek therapy or a healthy outlet for your frustration and aggression, because if you take it out on the people closest to you, they might just cut you out of their lives.

Call me crazy, but I don't think it's okay for anyone to get away with treating someone horribly just because they are related to them. Family members don't get a free pass to be rude just because they share our DNA, do they? I guess we each decide for ourselves.

I don't think there's a "right" or "wrong" answer here, but when I set boundaries for what behavior I'm willing to tolerate, it applies to everyone (whether it's a friend I've known for 20 years, someone I met moments ago, or my own flesh and blood).

If we are not kind to unkind people, we become them.

So, let's be kind to everyone without excuses. It's not that hard.

"When someone is mean to you,
they show you who they really are.
If you choose to be mean to them,
you reveal who you are.
Be kind."

Intervention

Two years after I took the monastic vows, trading all my worldly possessions for two sets of monk's robes, I moved into a monastery that was off the grid, remote, and blissfully quiet. One day, my friend Kim sent me a letter in which she wrote, "I understand why you love living there (who wouldn't?!), but how can you honor your vow to be of service to others if you cut yourself off from the rest of the world and keep yourself tucked away in the mountains?"

Kim didn't point out my hypocrisy because she's cruel or judgmental. She did it to shed light on what I couldn't see. My actions were not congruent with my words. There was no reason for me to get defensive because Kim wasn't offensive. I don't regret moving to the monastery, but I couldn't justify staying after Kim's intervention.

Non-Violent Communication (NVC) considers Unsolicited Advice a form of bullying, but Kim's comment wasn't unsolicited. I have an understanding with all my friends that being supportive of one another does not mean blindly cheering each other on.

In Buddhism, we take refuge in what are called The Three Jewels: the Buddha, the Dharma, and the Sangha (the teacher, the teachings, and other students on the path). My friends are my sangha, so if any of us are about to repeat a harmful cycle that we have clearly communicated we want to break, we welcome intervention. I wouldn't tell my buddy John to stop smoking, for example, because he never claimed that he wanted to stop, but I would definitely urge my friend Ashley to spend less money, since she had previously told me getting out of debt is her top priority. It's not about pushing my opinions on others; it's about supporting their intentions regardless of what I think.

Since you are on this path with me, this chapter is an intervention similar to what Kim offered me many years ago: it's an invitation to reflect on areas in our lives where we are being hypocritical; areas where we are not behaving in ways that are congruent with who we wish to be. We aren't always honest with ourselves about this because we often have too much shame or guilt around the decisions we make. Other times, we are oblivious that we are out of alignment.

I urge you not to look back on your past behavior and wonder why you've done what you've done. Instead, decide how you can live from this moment forward so that what you think, what you say, and what you do are all in harmony. Spoiler alert: you will likely need to change some of what you think, say, or do, before you can live a congruent life.

Congruence, consistency, and transparency require us to be vulnerable and honest with ourselves about our strengths and our shortcomings. Consider this your own intervention, which is defined as "The action of becoming intentionally involved in a difficult situation in order to improve it or to prevent it from getting worse."

Interventions like Black Lives Matter and the Me Too Movement have forced us to examine where we have unknowingly, unintentionally, or unconsciously been racist or failed to demand equality, even while claiming to believe in it. Wearing a monk's robes does not make someone a monk, just like a rosary does not make anyone a Catholic. In the words of Tyler Durden, "Sticking feathers up your butt does not make you a chicken."

A wise man once said, "There are no enlightened beings, there is only enlightened activity." The people we consider "enlightened" are just like you and me. They simply make enlightened activity part of their daily lives (that is to say they walk the talk).

Eventually, my own teachers looked at me and asked, "Timber, why do you need the robes? Why can't you just be the guy in town with the bright eyes?"

Indeed, why can't we all?

Composure

When things don't go well in our lives, we tend to project our frustration on the people closest to us when it's not their fault. This creates a problem in the relationship that wasn't there in the first place, adding one more issue to the list of things that aren't going well. That's why it's important to compartmentalize.

Your frustration with car trouble doesn't need to cause friction between you and your children, nor is it okay to allow the way your boss treats you to change the way you treat your spouse. Most of us like being in control, but the only thing we actually CAN control is the one thing we don't: our composure.

When family members visit for the holidays, imagine the following circumstances: the house will smell amazing from pies in the oven, and you will keep warm by the fireplace, but at least one of the guests will likely say something offensive, another might accidentally break something valuable, the neighbor's dog might bark all through dinner, there's a good chance someone will drink too much, talk politics, pick a fight, or be passive-aggressive enough to make snide comments about your house, the food, or say the "problem with the world today is people like you."

The above-scenario is just a snapshot of life, yet we don't have to allow the external chaos create disturbances within. My aunt is bothered by EVERYTHING—from the way people dress and talk, to the poor choices the government is making. There is always too much dressing on her salad, but never enough ice in her drink. She gets extra irritable when she's tired; she is grouchy if it's cold; and let's just say it's best to stay away from her when she's hungry. But if the weather is nice and she is well-rested, she can actually be pleasant and even kind. It's not just my aunt whose temperament is unpredictable, of course. We all feel joy, pain, anger, hunger, sympathy, irritation, excitement, and exhaustion, sometimes all in one evening, yet we rarely exercise the ability to maintain composure.

Controlling our attitude affects our experience, so it's surprising we expend so much energy trying to control the elements, but we don't pay enough attention to the tremendous difference a change in mindset can make.

Consider this chapter an invitation to stay calm and intentionally undisturbed. When I say "undisturbed," I'm not talking about numbness, apathy, indifference, or carelessness; I'm talking about emotional stability, which is the ability to care (even passionately), and have opinions (even strong ones), while calmly living in peace. It doesn't mean we don't proudly stand for what we value, it means we can quietly vote with our wallets to express our opinions, and we can support organizations that offer solutions to what we perceive to be problems.

Again, that's what we CAN do, but not necessarily what we actually practice. For all I know, you may be the guest at the dinner party who picks a fight or drinks too much, or the one who internalizes the external and lets it wreak havoc within. The question is: how do we compose ourselves when uncomfortable situations or disagreements arise, and why do we let our mood affect our manners?

Imagine my aunt maintaining composure, being kind to herself and to everyone around her (whether she is hungry, tired, hot, or cold). Not only would her own life improve, but so would the lives of everyone around her.

Composure is not a thought or a feeling, it's a practiced state of psychological stability. Composure is when we remain undisturbed by experiences, emotions, discomfort, or anything to which others react irrationally. The ability to remain calm and centered is not only fertile soil for wisdom and true freedom (both psychological and emotional), it is also the root of compassion. Even when outraged, once we compose ourselves, we can be a force for change fueled by constructive grace, not by destructive rage.

Remaining undisturbed by emotions or difficult situations does not mean we deny, suppress, or avoid our feelings (suppression of feelings is a form of non-acceptance and resistance). If you feel sad, you allow yourself to feel sad. Maintaining composure is about embracing the feeling without getting lost in it.

Read that again: **embrace the feeling without getting lost in it.**

Remaining composed is not the same as letting people walk all over you; it's actually the opposite. When you blame someone else for your behavior, THAT gives them all the power to manipulate you. Think about it: if you blame someone else for "making you angry," you essentially tell them that they have you wrapped around their little finger. But if you remain calm no matter what happens, and you stick to your conviction to be less reactive, to be more loving, and to remain peaceful regardless of what's going on inside or outside of you, THAT is your superpower. Claim it.

We LEARN composure while meditating in our peaceful little bubble; we PRACTICE composure at the dinner party when three people arrive late with unexpected guests; when the food is undercooked or burnt; when someone drops the pie on the floor and the cat eats just enough of it to get sick; when the power suddenly goes out; and when someone tells you that "the problem with the world is people like you" (perhaps specifically because you don't get angry like everyone else). Take it as a compliment.

Composure does not mean we pretend something doesn't hurt or bother us, nor do we dismiss anything with carelessness. If people hurt you and you feel angry, acknowledge the anger. But if you keep thinking about how terrible those people are, then your own thoughts will make you angrier. So, feel your temper, understand your temper, explain your temper, but don't lose your temper!

The Dalai Lama didn't say, "Only be kind to kind people when you are having a great day," he said, "Be kind whenever possible; it's always possible."

Echo Chamber

When I first decided to get healthy, it was difficult to spend time with friends who ate fast food all the time, not because they were "bad people" or because fast food is inherently "wrong," it simply wasn't conducive to my new lifestyle. Instead, I surrounded myself with people who regularly exercised, ate nutritious food, and kept stress to a minimum. They later told me that helping me find the path to better health strengthened their own resolve to stay on it.

When deciding to embark on a spiritual journey, however, cutting certain people out of our lives sounds like a logical parallel, but keeping ourselves in an echo chamber (where we only hear what we already believe repeated back to us), is actually detrimental to our spiritual growth. In a very real sense, those who challenge us actually teach us more than those who agree with us. They are not only beneficial to our growth, they are essential.

So, surround yourself with people who offer you a salad in one hand and a milkshake in the other, so to speak, because strength comes from actively choosing what is conducive to your journey, not from living in an echo chamber from which you've eliminated challenges.

Activism that brews in an echo chamber tends to be dangerously on the cusp between nonviolent protest and a riot. At some point, fighting for WHAT we believe is "right" turns into fighting to prove that WE are "right." That's when actions switch from altruistic endeavors to egotistic ones. The Buddha was an activist in that he actively encouraged people to think for themselves, but that is very different from telling people what to think.

This is exactly why we monks are discouraged from making the monastery our permanent home. We are urged to go back into the world of chaos, where our spirituality is challenged, not coddled, and where helping people find the spiritual path strengthens our own resolve to stay on it.

Guilt

There are two kinds of guilt: the unhealthy kind (what other people think you should feel based on their own expectations or on societal and cultural norms); and the healthy kind of guilt (genuine remorse that you feel from within).

Many people send me letters saying they are riddled with both types of guilt: the healthy kind (about things they have done and wish they hadn't), and the unhealthy kind (imposed upon them by others people—often relatives—who "make them feel guilty").

I put "make them feel" in quotes because I don't think anyone can "make you feel" something that you don't already feel (though some people certainly try).

When you actually DO feel guilty, isn't that a good sign that you regret certain behavior you would rather not repeat?

To better understand healthy guilt, I look back on my day each evening and give myself a daily report-card of sorts. Yesterday, for example, I flunked the Patience pop quiz, I got a 'B' on Kindness, I could have scored much higher than a 'C' in Self-Care, but I got a solid 'A' for Effort. Today, I get to try again. Healthy guilt is a wonderful internal compass for morals, ethics, and values, telling you when you have veered off the path. Each moment after that is an opportunity to redirect yourself toward true north.

This daily practice has a couple of benefits: 1) The act of acknowledging my missteps makes me less likely to repeat them, and 2) When I refrain from labeling myself a "bad person" just because I've made a mistake, I'm less likely to judge others as "bad" when they make a mistake. If it weren't for healthy guilt, I wouldn't take a closer look at some of my actions, and I might even fall into the trap of identifying with my mistakes as if they are all I am (such as a failure as opposed to someone who has failed; there is a big difference between the two).

Feeling remorseful is a fundamental part of Buddhism, which is all about breaking our detrimental cycles and embarking on a new path toward a more congruent and blissful life.

What helps me overcome the impulse to carry guilt from one day to the next is a frequent reminder that I am not what has happened in my life nor what I have done, I am who I choose to become today.

The person I was (the one who committed the act about which I feel guilty) no longer exists. This is a new day and a new me, and the new me knows better.

So, if you feel remorseful about something, that's great! Ask for forgiveness from whoever was involved (and also from yourself). If they choose to forgive you, great, but even if they don't, it isn't relevant for your internal process. Vow not to repeat that behavior again, and you can swiftly move past the debilitating feeling of guilt.

Now that you know how to distinguish between healthy guilt (remorse) and unhealthy guilt (the kind that someone else thinks you should feel), drop the unhealthy stuff right where you are. Most of what weighs you down isn't even yours to carry.

This may not be a magic guilt-be-gone potion, but if you practice this daily, it's close.

"To dwell in the present moment does not mean
you never think about the past
or responsibly plan for the future.
If you are firmly grounded in the present moment,
the past can be an object of inquiry.
You can attain many insights
by looking into the past
while staying grounded in the here and now."
— Thich Nhat Hanh

Let Go or Be Dragged

My friend Tanya complained to me about how stressful her job can be. She was thinking about looking for new work, so we tried to determine whether the problem was the job or her attitude about it. In other words: is it the load that's breaking her back, or is it the way she is carrying it?

Tanya, only in her mid-thirties, already struggles with anxiety and bouts of depression, along with sleep deprivation and fatigue. Because I know her well, I'm not sure the demands of the job are the problem. She's the kind of person who would be just as stressed working as a barista in a café as she is as a corporate executive on multi-million dollar projects. We talked about her tendency to respond to all work-related situations as matters of life-or-death.

We kept talking until we stumbled upon an interestingly opposing pattern: her ability NOT to stress in situations that would generally upset others. A fancy, brand new, glass coffee table shattered in her living room the previous week, and her immediate reaction was more *c'est la vie* than anything else. She actually found it funny.

This healthy response from one area of her life can be instructive in replacing the unhealthy reactions she has at work. That's why it was important for us to recognize that she CAN stay calm in a stressful situation. She can learn to respond to work-related situations the same way she kept her cool when the glass table broke, and then every aspect of her life would improve. Her assignment, so to speak, was to apply the same non-reactive perspective at work as she does in other situations.

The following week, Tanya called to tell me about a moment at work during which she was about to freak out, but then remembered the coffee table incident. She was able to tap into her choice to respond to the work situation the same way she did to the shattered glass. It is much easier for us to return to a place to which we've already been than to go somewhere for the first time. A calm response wasn't foreign to her, she just had to learn to implement it at work as she does at home. That's why it's key to recognize healthy patterns as well as unhealthy ones. We can then exercise those muscles until "letting go" becomes the new pattern.

We go through life like we're driving down a highway. We set the cruise control for our ideal speed, but we get frustrated when there is a slow driver or an unexpected turn ahead that forces us to slow down. But the problem isn't other drivers or the road, it's our mentality that the world should revolve around our preferences. Getting rid of that mentality is the key to freedom.

I actually think the same stressful and annoying situations keep recurring in our lives as new opportunities for us to respond differently than the way we did when they happened before. If you no longer want to get upset when somebody cuts you off on the freeway, but you slip and get upset again, don't worry; someone will cut you off again soon enough, and you will get to try a more patient approach then. Each instance is an invitation to put mindfulness into practice. As Pema Chödrön says, "A lesson will repeat itself until you learn it."

Everything (and I mean EVERYTHING), becomes more enjoyable when we let go of the illusions we have about how the world "should" be and how people "should" behave. Just because the situation is stressful doesn't mean we have to be stressed. Our response is the one thing we can control.

I used to live and drive in Los Angeles, where it often takes a half hour to travel just five miles by car. Instead of getting upset, I chose to listen to audiobooks and podcasts, which is how I arrived everywhere stress-free.

"Let go or be dragged,
the choice is yours."

Response-Ability

As a kid, I used to cry in my room after my parents beat me, and I would wait for them to come back to comfort me.

In elementary school, after kids bullied me, the teacher would pull them by the ear and tell them to apologize to me.

Through these childhood experiences, I developed an illogical expectation that whoever broke something would come back to fix it. But we can't sit around waiting for the person who caused the hurt to also be the one to console us.

If other people upset me, the problem isn't other people; it's me. And that's a good thing because I can do something about me; I can't change anybody else.

Choosing to get angry, frustrated, hurt, or upset, is a complete waste of our power, which is why we end up feeling powerless. To add insult to injury, we then expect the people who were careless with us to do the mending. It's like getting upset with a puppy for peeing on the floor, and then expecting the puppy to clean it up.

I've known people who waited decades for an apology that never came, clinging to their pain and resentment as if it's precious.

We decide for how long we are going to let what hurt us haunt us.

Even if the wound itself is not your fault, healing from it is your Response-Ability (the ability to choose your response).

> "People are to be loved, things are to be used.
> The reason the world is in chaos is
> because things are being loved,
> and people are being used."
> — The Dalai Lama

No Parking

In what is normally a quiet, seaside community, the neighbors across the street from where I used to live had a large gathering in their house one day, which meant more cars than usual were parked all over the neighborhood. One of those vehicles partially blocked my next-door neighbor's driveway, which made it difficult (but not impossible) for her to get in and out of her garage.

I don't believe in telling anyone what they "should" or "shouldn't" do, so regardless of the situation, I believe a peaceful person responds to situations peacefully; an angry person reacts angrily; a pessimist assumes the worst in people; and an optimist tends to give everyone the benefit of the doubt (maybe even to a fault).

When people try to justify how they respond to certain situations in their lives (be it at home, at work, or out in public), they tend to over-explain the details as if looking for some sort of permission or validation that their behavior is all right. We all want to hear good news about our bad habits.

Most people blame how they behave on what happens around them, but I'd like us to consider how much of what happens around us is shaped by how we behave.

As for the car blocking the driveway, how would you respond? Would you simply let it go, knowing full well the driver will soon leave, and what has never happened on your block before will likely never happen again? Would you leave a note on their windshield alerting the driver to the inconvenience they've caused? Would you knock on the door and ask them to move the car? Would you call the police or a tow truck? Or would you immediately erect a large, homemade sign in the front yard with big, capital letters painted in red, spelling, NO PARKING, which is what my neighbor chose to do. What would you do?

It turned out the gathering across the street was a wake for a deceased relative. The driver who blocked the driveway was elderly and understandably distracted considering the occasion. Though this does not excuse the infraction, the driver had no ill-intentions.

Would finding out the reason for the gathering across the street change your reaction? What if it was a Super Bowl party? What if it was a baby shower? Would the neighbor's race, religion, or political leanings make a difference?

Why we behave the way we do is actually not dependent on outside circumstances, it has everything to do with who WE are. Details about the driver are irrelevant, as is the reason for the gathering. Once we decide what kind of person we choose to be, those things don't matter. If we are committed to being kind, for example, then we will be kind in every situation. This does not mean we roll over and let people walk all over us, unless that's the kind of person we decide to be. It's entirely our decision. The little kid in us wants to say, "Yeah, but..." or "He started it," while the adult in us struggles to take control of the situation.

I'm not asking you "What Would Jesus Do?" or "What Would Buddha Do?" I'm asking "What would YOU do?"

If you were to put up a sign in your front lawn, what would it say? "No Parking?" "Stay Off My Lawn?" or "Have a Nice Day?"

We may not be in the business of putting up signs, but we DO post on social media, and what we choose to post says a lot.

"It's okay to be angry,
it's not okay to be cruel.
If you can't control the feeling,
control the emotion.
Emote kindness.
Always."

It's Not You, It's Me

Have you ever noticed that some of the things you consider irritating are pleasant for other people? Hot weather, classical music, laughing children, long drives, thunderstorms, gardening, data entry, and so on. Someone is looking forward to what you regularly try to avoid.

When I get annoyed by someone blasting their car stereo in a residential neighborhood, I remind myself that I used to do the same thing when I was younger. And when cigarette smoke disgusts me, I recall my own Marlboro days until my judgy-wudgy attitude dissolves. It's important to keep ourselves in check so that we don't start thinking our way of being is somehow superior.

You will only be surrounded by annoying people and frustrating situations until you learn not to get annoyed or frustrated. We need to stop blaming outside forces for our own lack of internal peace. It's not about getting everyone to live in line with what we think is right, it's about staying peaceful regardless of what's going on.

Personal responsibility is not just accountability for the way our lives have turned out so far, but also for the perspectives with which we continue viewing the world today. We need to stop expecting perfection from others as if we can possibly offer it in return.

Consider the likelihood that the windchime you think is peaceful in your garden is perceived as inconsiderate and presumptuous by a neighbor who hates the sound. Your idea of "normal" is ridiculously absurd to someone else. And never assume that you are any less irritating than the people you try to avoid.

If I get aggravated by something you do, it's not your fault that I haven't learned how not to get annoyed. You are actually my greatest teacher, and from the moment I start looking at you from that perspective, all I want to do is thank you, not kick you in the teeth ☺

It's not you, it's me.

Bad Mood

I am often asked if I'm always happy, and I think it's important to distinguish between being happy and being in a good mood. I believe happiness is our natural state, a sort of baseline, but that happiness is susceptible to fluctuations.

When I recently had a falling out with one of my distributors, the conversation turned ugly. I instinctively wanted to fall back into an old pattern rooted in the fallacy that if things are already bad, I might as well make them worse.

For example, when I was growing up, ice cream used to give me a stomachache, so I made it a rule to only eat ice cream if my stomach was already hurting (if things are bad, might as well make them worse). Now, even though I know better, the old impulse to "make things worse when they are bad" still rears its ugly head.

The moment I hung up the phone with the distributor, my mind raced with destructive impulses to make a bad situation worse (pick your poison of choice). Instead, I decided to meditate even though it was the last thing I wanted to do right then. That much-needed time to reflect, however, clarified for me that while I definitely needed to blow off steam, there are healthy and unhealthy ways to do it. The pause I took between impulse and response was where I navigated toward the kind of person I want to be, and away from my old habitual reactions.

I decided to go for a swim at the local gym. On the way there, more options presented themselves: I could listen to *Versions of Violence* by Alanis Morissette at full volume (which would just add fuel to the fire because that's just the kind of song it is), or I could tune-in to *The Moth Radio Hour* (a podcast of people sharing personal stories), which would replace my own narrative so I could cool off.

We all do different things to escape reality (drugs, sex, food, video games, etc.), but I find that escaping into someone else's story gives me enough distance from mine to get a clearer perspective.

The decision to end the business relationship with the distributor wasn't ideal, but neither was the relationship in the first place or it wouldn't have ended. When I looked at it that way, I stopped feeling "wronged," and started feeling liberated, free, and unburdened. Nothing changed except my attitude. And just like that, I was back to being happy AND in a good mood.

It's empowering to remind myself that when I'm angry, for example, I'm CHOOSING to be angry. Then I can ask myself, "Timber, why are you choosing to feel this? It sucks! There are so many other ways you can choose to feel." I immediately laugh at my self for thinking in the third person, then choose a new feeling to replace the anger.

We can choose to feel happy or crappy, but it's our choice either way.

What do you choose?

> "Just like you can't see your reflection in boiling water,
> you can't see clearly in a state of anger.
> Simmer down.
> Look again."

Trauma Response

In my mid-forties, I had a realization that I was reluctant to talk to my friends about, let alone share publicly. But nothing I experience is unique to me since many of us share a common story, so I'm going on record here because this recent revelation might shed some light on your own journey as well.

For as long as I can remember, I have avoided being around children, hanging out with friends when their kids were present, and even regularly saying that I hated children!

While "hate" is a strong word (that I typically only use when talking about bean sprouts), this hatred toward children felt somehow justified when I thought it was simply because kids tend to be loud and I am sensitive to noise. But nobody likes a screaming child on an airplane or in a restaurant, yet we can't blame a kid for being a kid. From the stories I've heard, I was a baby from hell, constantly screaming and throwing tantrums.

After recently spending time with a few kids ranging in age from 5 to 12, we had fun together even though they were very loud. We joked around, played games, ran around to the point of exhaustion, and I barely recognized myself. That was until the kids' parents showed up. Within seconds, the parents started criticizing their kids, telling them how to behave, bargaining with them to stop doing this and that, shouting at them to quiet down, and berating them with the all-too-familiar phrase, "Don't use that tone with me!"

I immediately felt uncomfortable, so I removed myself from the situation. I wondered if perhaps children aren't the problem after all; maybe it's being around parents that bothers me. But why? I constantly talk about maintaining our inner peace regardless of what's going on around us, so what is this specific and persistent aversion all about?

When I traced back the events of the day, I realized that I don't hate children and I don't hate their parents. What I hate is my childhood! THAT'S what I've been avoiding all these years. Staying away from children was simply a trauma response, not a solution; it was a way to dodge any and all triggers of my own past experience, buried deep inside, but in there just the same.

A Course in Miracles states: "I am never upset for the reason I think." In other words, nothing in the external world causes our fear, guilt, shame, or hurt, it's all internal. This realization liberates us from being a victim and empowers us to claim responsibility for our state of mind. What a relief!

This felt like a profound turning point for me, much like the phobia I overcame and wrote about in the *Buddhist Boot Camp* chapter entitled "Rewriting the Stories we Tell Ourselves."

My story about children and parents was long overdue for a rewrite. I am grateful to have had this experience, even though it was painful to relive the condemnation, the harsh discipline, the fear of a raised hand in violence, the yelling, punishing, and constant disapproval. I wonder how much more is buried behind layers of pain. The good news is that I am no longer afraid to look because I know letting it go will lead to growth.

We are never upset for the reason we think. The upsetting situation is a gift. It is an invitation to reevaluate our existing limiting and narrow beliefs that are working against us. While it's unfortunate that sometimes pain is our greatest teacher, if that's what it takes, bring it on! I'd rather deal with the discomfort of change than the agony of staying the same.

I wish you growth, insight, and relief from suffering.

"When suffering knocks on the door of your life,
may you glimpse its eventual gifts."
—John O'Donohue

Multi-Faceted

I'm going to start by describing a scenario I've shared in the past, both in previous writings and public talks. Then I'm going to take the same scenario to the next level and see if it makes you uncomfortable, which usually indicates I'm doing my job (raising awareness of our own hidden biases). After we acknowledge them, we can work on letting them go.

Imagine you and I are walking down the street together, and suddenly a big dog starts running toward us. I absolutely love dogs, so I'm thrilled and think this dog is adorable. If you were perhaps attacked by a dog at some point, you might think this is a very scary situation. So, is the dog cute or scary? Well, Buddhism teaches us that the dog is neither cute nor scary—it's just a dog. We, on the other hand, are meaning-making-machines who assign value to everything we see, creating our own unique experience. Whether the experience is pleasant or unpleasant is completely up to us, regardless of whether our perception is even accurate.

To get to the core of why bias and segregation is so detrimental to us, I now want you to imagine walking down the same street, but this time, instead of a dog, you see a young man wearing a shirt bearing a racist symbol on the front. What experience does that trigger in you? What if it's an elderly man? What if it's a woman? Let's forget the racist symbol and consider what response would be triggered if you were to see a soldier in uniform walking down the street, a doctor in scrubs, a firefighter in full gear, or a monk in robes? What sort of thoughts and assumptions get triggered then?

In reality, the person in front of you is just a person, multi-faceted and unlike anyone else. But we impulsively assign meaning and labels to everything we witness, which triggers all sorts of emotions within us. All too often, unfortunately, too many people act on those emotions, unreliable and inaccurate as they may be.

While I envision a world without labels that segregate us based on ethnicity, religion, age, income, skin color, sexual orientation, political affiliation, gender identity, or physical ability, many people are extremely protective of those labels because their very identity is wrapped up in them. That's why my utopian dream of living without labels is unrealistic. The people who identify with their labels see my suggestion to drop the labels altogether as a threat, essentially asking them to deny who they are, even though my intention is for us to see ourselves and others as much more than the labels we wear.

I have no idea how old some of my best friends are, how much money they make, or for whom they voted in the last election. I don't think it matters. Some of these friends have remained in my life through various stages, whether I was working in the corporate world or the graveyard shift at a gas station, whether I was living in a condo downtown or in a monastery. They were my friends when I was drinking, smoking, meditating, single, married, financially secure, or barely making ends meet. So, despite the fact that those things don't matter, some people make them matter.

I acknowledge that it's possible some labels offered us a sense of comfort and even pride during a certain time in our lives. But later in life, the same label that brought us comfort before, can suddenly segregate and separate us, maybe even confine us into a little box of our own making.

Imagine labeling all dogs as scary. Imagine labeling yourself as a screw-up. Imagine labeling yourself as young, or healthy, or able-bodied. I am many things, and not one of them defines me. This is true for myself and for everyone else.

The question to ask ourselves is: Do our labels work FOR us or AGAINST us?

Only you can answer that for yourself.

Bouncer

I was in my 20's at the height of the 90's club scene. We either spent the night standing in line with cash in hand to pay the cover charge to get out of the cold and onto the dance floor, or we cut to the front of the line because the bouncer knew we were on the guest list as friends of the manager, the bartender, or the DJ.

Young and broke but addicted to bass, we did everything we could to secure a spot on that guest list. In our eyes, the bouncer at each club was right up there with Saint Peter protecting the Pearly Gates of heaven. The Gods spun records, and the bouncers were respected because they had the authority, the power, and the muscle to kick you out or to let you in.

Bouncers were also responsible for making sure the male-to-female ratio inside each club was balanced, and in some extreme cases, their job was to only allow the "pretty people" inside.

Why am I telling you this? Because many people tell me they feel like failures at meditation when random thoughts still show up. Silly as it may sound, I picture a bouncer in my head deciding which thoughts are free to join the party, which have to stand outside, and which are banned for life. Many different thoughts show up, but that doesn't mean they all get to dance!

Back in the day, some people who were desperate to get into the club resorted to extreme measures, which is what the silly song *DJ Girl* was all about. The lyrics consisted of a conversation between a club bouncer and a very determined groupie carrying records, pleading to get inside. "I'm with the DJ. I'm with the DJ, okay?"

Much like her, unwelcomed thoughts wear a disguise or use a fake ID—anything to gain entry into our minds. The bouncer's job is to stick to the names on the guest list or the given criteria. Do you see how useful having a bouncer like that in our heads can be to keep certain thoughts from stealing the spotlight?

Also, be on the lookout for destructive thoughts lurking outside the backdoor trying to sneak in behind other thoughts (the way people enter apartment buildings when someone else gets buzzed inside).

We need to be vigilant and never slack, because once a thought gets in, it can be very difficult to get it out. When I recently shared this metaphor with a local congregation, the minister said he's from the generation when club managers tapped you on the shoulder while you were dancing to politely ask you to leave the dance floor. You didn't have to go home, but you couldn't stay in the spotlight.

If you are not a club kid, simply imagine going through airport security, where they decide what is allowed onto the plane and what is not. We all have baggage, for example, but if someone shows up with more than what's allowed, they either pay extra, or they have to leave it behind. Use whatever metaphor works for you, but get in touch with the bouncer within.

In all seriousness, write up a guest list and stand guard.

We need to set clear parameters for our thoughts. Otherwise, we risk letting expired beliefs, hostile opinions, and disruptive distractions to live rent-free in our heads. We can't allow sick thoughts to infect our healthy thoughts by letting them dance together.

I offer these playful visuals because I seriously use them myself. Instead of playing the victim of our thoughts as if we have no control over them, this role of gate keeper, bouncer, or security guard is one of the most important jobs you will ever have.

So, get to work. Your happiness depends on it.

> "The happiness of your life
> depends upon the quality of your thoughts.
> Guard accordingly.
> Entertain no notions unsuitable to virtue
> and reasonable nature."
> —Marcus Aurelius

The Blame Game

Tempting as it may be to blame unfavorable circumstances for our anguish, most of our suffering is not caused by other people or situations, it's caused by the way we react to them. The thought "This shouldn't be happening to me" sparks our anger, anxiety, despair, and hopelessness; those feelings make any situation worse.

That simple thought "This shouldn't be happening," takes what would otherwise be a less-than-ideal situation, and turns it into devastation. Asking questions such as, "Why me?" stems from looking at the world through victim mentality. Thich Nhat Hanh said, "When we learn how to suffer, we suffer much less." The pain of life is inevitable, but suffering is optional.

Realistically speaking, many circumstances in life won't be ideal, comfortable, or convenient. We have all gone through experiences that fluctuated from the seemingly unbearable to absolutely incredible. Resistance to that fluctuation leads to a lifelong struggle with everything and everyone around us. Alternatively, we can navigate through the inevitable twists and turns with grace and acceptance. The first secret to doing this skillfully is acknowledging that those twists and turns are inevitable. Don't kid yourself by thinking life is going to be "smooth sailing" at any point; it won't be.

There will always be something or someone testing our patience. We can either learn what the situation is trying to teach us (patience), or we can keep blaming our emotional state on our relatives, coworkers, presidents, or other drivers on the road. Blaming others may give your story a "bad guy," but it will take a toll on your mental and physical health. Other people are not the problem, it's your short fuse that is a bit of a joy-killer.

There is nothing inherently wrong with Mondays or with wrinkles; the problem is our attitude about those things. I'm not suggesting we become numb or witness what we think is unjust and do nothing about it. I have simply noticed how much more peacefully we can live when we remain peaceful (sound obvious, doesn't it?).

There are billions of people in the world; don't let just one of them ruin your day (and definitely don't let that one person be you).

We have all been lied to, cheated on, overworked, underpaid, wronged, misunderstood, and underappreciated, yet we are still here; we are not broken.

In fact, we will likely be wronged again, the invitation is for us to handle it skillfully, rationally, and peacefully in order to improve the quality of our lives. It's why you are reading this book in the first place, isn't it? So, stop blaming other people for how you choose to feel. It's unfair to them, and it undermines your own empowerment.

> "Our life is shaped by our mind; we become what we think.
> Joy follows a pure thought like a shadow that never leaves."
> — The Buddha

It's All in My Head

The other night, I dreamt that I was trapped in a crowded room with a bunch of angry people screaming at each other. I didn't have my noise-canceling headphones with me or any other way to escape. I woke up from that nightmare experiencing a full-blown anxiety attack, sweating profusely, with my heart pounding so fast I couldn't catch my breath. Physically, I wasn't in a loud, crowded room; I was comfortably tucked under the covers in my quiet bedroom. So, why was I freaking out?

Where I am physically and where I am in my mind have nothing to do with one another. That experience of having a panic attack while alone in my room because of loud noises in my head (yet also being able to stand in the middle of Manhattan during rush hour and stay as calm as can be), just reaffirmed for me that where I am in my mind is far more important than what's going on around me.

Through repetition, we can train our minds to remain calm in any situation. Always staying calm might not be the most appropriate response in a true emergency, but I'd rather be too calm than react to daily inconveniences as if each was a natural disaster.

It's amazing that we need to take driver's education, get a license, and buy insurance to drive a car, yet we get no training on how to use the most powerful tool we have: our minds.

Let's bring awareness to where our thoughts go when left on autopilot. I'm still training myself to pause whenever I feel uneasy, breathe deeply, and ask myself, "What thought can I choose in this moment that would be more beneficial?"

Reclaiming that navigational power is a huge step.

Let's take it together.

Is It True Love?

People often ask me how Buddhism can be simultaneously centered around love and non-attachment.

Love and attachment are not the same thing. In fact, they are opposites. Attachment is fear-based, not love-based. Attachment is selfish, not selfless. True love is liberating, not confining. And if love isn't unconditional, then it isn't love at all.

If you only love someone because they love you back (or you expect they always will), then you are in love with being loved, not with the other person. There is nothing inherently wrong with that, but it isn't love; it is a self-centered need to feel important, admired, and cared-for. True love has nothing to do with possession, and it doesn't come with any contingencies.

While your love for someone can be unconditional, being in a relationship with them can most certainly have conditions. Whether it's blood relation or romantic chemistry, it doesn't always imply compatibility. In the past, I have said to numerous people that I couldn't imagine my life without them. Yet here I am, after years of not having them in my life for one reason or another, and I'm perfectly fine. This has taught me to be less melodramatic and more honest with myself and with others.

I still love deeply, but without attachment. This actually makes my love stronger and more intense, not because it lasts forever, but because I realize nothing ever does. It allows me to appreciate each moment and each person that much more.

Would you continue loving someone if they stopped loving you, or is your love contingent upon them loving you back?

Are the people in your life filling a void, or are they enriching a life that you already love?

Watch Your Language

When I sat down to write my memoir in 2015, it felt accurate but strange to describe my childhood as difficult, traumatic, tragic, or unfair, because I obviously survived it. I decided to experiment with recounting the events and experiences from my past but to do it without using any adjectives. That's how I managed to recall the past while sidestepping the slippery slope of victim mentality and preventing a likely free-fall into the abyss of depression.

My friend compares the pain of grief to a large hole in the ground that she kept falling into. The hole is still there, but she has learned to walk around it. This practice doesn't deny, ignore, or even minimize the past; it still acknowledges everything that happened, but it doesn't sensationalize it, which makes a huge difference.

Some people take issue with the notion that time heals all wounds. I evaluate emotional healing the same way doctors monitor patients after a medical procedure: by gauging the pain's intensity, frequency, and duration. Grief can feel really heavy at first, and I still don't know if it actually gets lighter with time, or if we grow strong enough to handle the extra weight. Either way, the pain's intensity, frequency, and duration is reduced as time goes on. I wouldn't say we ever fully heal (there will always be a scar), but it definitely doesn't hurt as much anymore.

We can speak or write about any experience from our past (breakups, injustice, or loss), without any anger, resentment, or even judgment. I equate it to stepping out of a movie theater and explaining to a friend what happened on the screen; I can describe each scene, but I don't have any emotional reaction or attachment to it because it's over and done.

As long as the narrator in your head keeps labeling what happened "devastating" or "traumatic," you will continue to be devastated or traumatized. This can ruin your present and your future.

Next time you share a story of past experiences, try doing it without adjectives; the story will still hold true without being sensationalized.

By tapping into the strength with which you made it through everything in your life so far, you access the same strength that will carry you through whatever comes next.

I use this technique when working with those who suffer from PTSD and are determined to move past it, but it's an exercise from which we can all benefit. I'm sure you can think of a past experience that can use rephrasing. Perhaps change the descriptive narrative from "horrible" or "tragic" to "challenging." It's still true, it's just not as heavy.

We are not defined by what has happened in our lives nor anything we have done; we are who we choose to become... TODAY.

The past is in your head, the future is in your hands.

"If we don't heal from what hurt us,
we end up bleeding on people who didn't cut us."

Understanding Hatred

If I asked you to list five red items as quickly as possible, you would probably say, "roses, tomatoes, fire trucks, stop signs," and maybe "Rudolph's nose." That's because we compulsively file everything we see and experience into groups, categories, and types.

Ever since infancy, this advanced mental filing system makes the world less overwhelming for us to process. We notice something, we cross-reference it with everything that is already familiar to us, and we quickly label it as either harmless or dangerous, cute or scary, and so on. But where do those labels come from?

One problem is that we label everything unconsciously and automatically as individuals, and another problem is that we do it collectively as a society. We use preassigned labels for whatever we don't understand by looking at society's preexisting categories as a guide. These values may have been set by our parents, our close circle of friends, or worse yet, the Internet.

Many of our thoughts, opinions, and beliefs are founded on information we subconsciously receive from sources as unreliable as the grapevine. I recently heard someone say, "The people with the most money have the biggest megaphones, but it doesn't mean they have the most interesting or accurate things to say."

We witness this whenever a celebrity recommends a product that becomes an overnight success. There is nothing inherently wrong with influencers like that, but there's a difference between leaders who tell you what to think and those who invite you to think for yourself. We somehow simultaneously insist on referring to ourselves as independent thinkers, yet we love it when others do the thinking for us. As Björk sang, "There is no logic to human behavior."

When we were teenagers, many of us became attached to popular beliefs in order to appear popular. But as adults, I think it's our inherent responsibility to question those beliefs. If we never step outside of our small circle of friends and family, we end up living in a bubble, agreeing with everyone who agrees with us and unfriending or disowning anyone who does not.

Labeling and categorizing may sound harmless, effective, and even necessary (which it can certainly be at times), but not if we don't know the source of our information. Investigating the origin of external stimuli (like the news) is something I think we do a little more these days, but it's equally imperative to also question what's behind the source of our existing opinions, because it could very well be the ego. That's why I often remind myself not to believe everything I think.

The ego can be dangerous because it is selfish enough to justify hatred and violence as virtues. Driven by its lust for power, the ego considers the harm it causes as somehow superior to the harm caused by others, without pausing to realize that causing harm only leads to more harm. This was glaringly obvious to me during a recent conversation with a so-called peace activist (we'll call him Rob), who was far from peaceful and bordering on hostile. He insisted there's a difference between a neo-Nazi who wants him dead because he is black or gay, for example, and him wanting to kill that neo-Nazi. The reality is that even terrorists believe they are fundamentally good. It's our behavior that inevitably reflects the hate within each of us, often disguised as passion, faulty logic, or a helpful coping mechanism. We hate bigots, racists, and fundamentalists, but why? Because they hate us? How does that make sense?

This was one of the most challenging perspectives to hold when I was growing up in Israel. The Israeli kids were practically raised to hate Palestinians, while Palestinians were raised to hate Israelis. We hated them because they hated us (and they followed the same dangerous rationale). When I moved to the United States and befriended my first Palestinian, we both laughed at the absurdity of it all (even though it wasn't funny, and still isn't).

I think segregation is to blame. As Ani DiFranco said, "I was five years old when they showed me a picture of three oranges and a pear. They asked me, 'Which one is different and does not belong?' They taught me that different is wrong." That's exactly what segregation does.

So, I asked Rob if he had unconsciously contributed to our segregated world in his own way, and although he didn't like admitting it, he said that having a special channel on TV for black people (BET) probably isn't a good idea (or that it was perhaps necessary at a time but is outdated today). He also said that going to gay clubs may have made sense a few years ago as a safe space for him to go, but all the clubs nowadays further segregate the community into more sub-communities, often pitted against one another. He laughed and said that instead of simply categorizing movies as Comedy, Drama, or Suspense, for example, Netflix now has an LGBTQIA category. For whose benefit does that segregation exist?

There is a difference between categorizing apple varieties in the grocery store and the aforementioned categorization on Netflix. One is rooted in hatred and segregation (and I'm not talking about the green apples versus the red).

Here is my question for you: "Is there a difference between the hatred that the neo-Nazi has toward Rob and the hatred that Rob has toward the neo-Nazi?"

In both cases, the hatred stems from fear of the unknown, panic that one person's way of life oppresses the other's, and a deep-rooted need to defend and protect the values that each holds at any cost. Even if one becomes the very instrument of death and misery to defend those values, he still feels he is in the "right." And why is that? Because in our compulsive need to label everything as either "wrong" or "right," what do you think we label ourselves?

We think we are right, of course, every time!

To better understand hatred, we must first be honest about where it hides within each of us. It sometimes dresses up as bigotry, discrimination, prejudice, self-righteousness, preference, favoritism, bias, convenience, or partiality, but it's there.

Once we see it in ourselves, we can recognize it all around us, and then we can stop feeding the hate-based segregation that we've been condoning in our lives without even realizing it (like when we mindlessly support businesses and policies that benefit from systematically keeping us separate instead of unified).

As Martin Luther King Jr. brilliantly summarized, "Darkness cannot drive out darkness; only light can do that. And hate cannot drive out hate; only love can do that."

> "How easy it is
> to see your brother's faults;
> how hard it is
> to face your own.
> You mock his,
> but yours you hide.
> Dwelling on your brother's faults
> multiplies your own."
> — The Buddha

Eight Minutes and Forty-Six Seconds

When I'm on a book tour, I couch-surf with different host families along the way. A few years ago, an elderly and physically disabled host was generous enough to have me in his home for a couple of nights. He wanted to attend my book talk, but he had trouble seeing at night, so he asked that I drive us to and from the event in his car, which more easily accommodated him.

We were so engaged in conversation on the drive back to his house that I missed a turn. He casually said, "Oh, we were supposed to turn left back there," so I made a U-turn in the middle of the street. He gripped the door handle with one hand, grabbed the center console with the other, and screamed, "WHAT ARE YOU DOING!?"

His reaction surprised me. I pulled over and said, "I turned the car around because you said I had driven past your street." He just looked at me and said, "Oh, you don't know about DWB, do you?"

DWB (Driving While Black) means he would never attempt to get away with the kind of maneuver that I just pulled. "If you were black," he told me, "and a certain type of cop saw you do that, you'd get pulled over, have your head slammed against the hood of the car, arms handcuffed behind your back, and likely get arrested."

That night I learned the difference between white privilege and white ignorance. I was ignorant of my privilege, yes, but Privilege (with a capital P), is when you think something isn't a problem just because it doesn't affect you.

Racism is a problem bigger than job inequality or persons of color serving prison sentences four times longer whites who commit the same crime. Racism is bigger than my parents forbidding me from dating anyone in my teens who wasn't Jewish, to which I obviously rebelled by dating the darkest-skinned Christian I could find.

Racism is a matter of life or death.

I hosted an online discussion about the murder of George Floyd, a black man choked to death by a police officer who knelt on his neck for eight minutes and forty-six seconds while George cried, "I can't breathe!" Three other officers stood by and watched as George's body became unresponsive. When I posted information about the online discussion, many claimed I had no business talking about racism because I'm not black (which is a fair point, though I've had my share of death threats, hate crimes, and even swastikas carved on my locker in High School simply because I'm not white). Other people said it would be irresponsible for me to ignore what's going on and pretend nothing happened (which is also a fair point). Others understood my effort as an ally to bring mindfulness to a very sensitive and horrifying situation.

I felt everyone's rage coursing through my own veins. The protests and riots reminded me of the aftermath from the beating of Rodney King in 1991, and I was furious that we've made so little progress in the 30 years since then.

This brutal crime was videotaped and caused outrage all over the world. Being enraged was the most appropriate response, so my fury was certainly justified, but I had to keep reminding myself that if I start hating the haters, I become a hater myself.

My mantra became: "Feel your temper, understand your temper, but don't lose your temper." Let's not stoop to the very violence we wish to eradicate.

As we chant in Zen temples every morning, "Greed, Hatred, and Ignorance rise endlessly; I vow to abandon them." I have said this before and I'll say it again: We are taught to be tolerant and accepting, but tolerance does not mean accepting what is harmful.

Regardless of your personal opinions about the murder of George Floyd, I want you to set a timer for eight minutes and forty-six seconds to grasp how long that is.

Eight minutes and forty-six seconds. Let each second sink in.

The Platinum Rule

When my friend was hired to work the reception desk of a popular hotel, prior to answering phones and booking rooms, they had him spend a month doing everything from housekeeping to room service, laundry, bellhop, and so on. I used to work at a restaurant with the same philosophy, where supervisors were made, not hired. The idea was that it's crucial for everyone on staff to understand everybody else's job. Whenever a manager asked for something to be done, they knew exactly what was involved and how much time it would take. There was camaraderie amongst everyone working together toward the same goal rather than working "for" one another in an endless power struggle.

While working in a law firm, it was frowned upon for lawyers to have lunch with their paralegals, or for the secretaries to fraternize with the receptionists. I'm just using these examples of segregation to show how lack of connection leads to a greater social gap between us, almost like a caste system that nobody talks about.

The golden rule with which many of us were raised to treat others the way we wish to be treated, is an outdated model. The platinum rule, on the other hand, invites us to treat others the way THEY want to be treated (and we can never know how they want to be treated unless we ask).

If we don't get curious about other perspectives, we run the risk of thinking we are actually right about something, or worse yet, thinking we are superior to someone else. I love the joke that one day scientists are going to discover what's at the center of the universe, and many people will be very disappointed to find out it isn't them.

While we are wired for connection with one another, we are unfortunately programmed for protection from one another. This creates miles of separation between us, which explains why so many of us feel alone and disconnected from each other.

When my car broke down in a foreign country, and I was stranded on the side of the road with a dead cell phone, all I wanted was for someone (anyone) to pull over to help (by either calling a tow truck or maybe offering me a bottle of water while I stood there in the afternoon sun). I watched all the passing motorists zoom by and longed for some connection with anyone kind enough to pull over.

If you were in that situation and someone pulled over to offer their help, you wouldn't ask them who they voted for, if they believed in Jesus, Moses, or Muhammad, or if they identified as male, female, or neither. You would just say, "Thank You."

When it comes to connection, none of the stuff we think matters ends up mattering at all. Perhaps more importantly, if you are the one driving and you see someone broken-down on the side of the road, help them. It doesn't matter who they voted for, if they believe in Jesus, Moses, or Muhammad, or if they identify as male, female, or neither. Just offer them a bottle of water or a ride to the nearest service station; whatever they need. Ask.

I'm about to say something I might later regret not being able to articulate more skillfully: the problem is not that the things that separate us are stupid; what's stupid is the fact that they separate us.

One of my teachers used to say, "Instead of meditating for 30 minutes on peace and relieving suffering in the world, meditate for 15 minutes, and then get off your cushion, roll up your sleeves, and use the other 15 minutes actually relieving suffering in the world."

We witness people coming together for earthquake and hurricane rescue efforts, right? But we don't need a disaster to force us to think outside of ourselves, do we?

Connection is the key to empathy. Let's use it to come together because of our common humanity.

"Humankind. Be Both."

Boundaries

We may not want to admit it, but we all care what other people think about us to some degree. It's why we wear or don't wear certain clothes, fix our hair, refrain from certain behavior in public, etc. And while some consideration and awareness of our surrounding is imperative, making other people's opinion of us the driving force behind our decisions can become problematic.

We protect what's important to us, but since we consider so many things important (and it's impossible to protect everything), at some point, something's gotta give.

Gandhi said, "Your actions convey your priorities." And sadly, many people care most about other people's perception of them, so curating and protecting their image has become the priority.

Out of fear of being judged, we forget that we can be kind with a good heart and still say No to people (including family members, friends, employers, and neighbors). Setting boundaries is crucial to ensure we don't end up living our entire lives just to impress others.

Before we can draw boundaries, however, we need to define our priorities. If my priority on Sunday is to finish writing an essay when a friend asks me to help him move, it's okay for me to say, "I can only come for an hour," or even say, "I'd rather not, but can I have some pizza delivered to your house around noon while you pack?" The point is not to feel forced to lie, guilty, stuck, cornered, helpless, or fearful of what someone might think of us if we prioritize something other than what they think is more important.

Take personal responsibility for your time, money, energy, schedule, and well-being. Without those boundaries, people might drain you, but it wouldn't even be their fault. How are they to know that they have crossed a line if you didn't set it in the first place? And if you DID set a boundary but didn't stick to it, keep in mind that what you allow is what will continue. You teach people how to treat you.

There was a sign in my old office that read, "Your lack of planning is not my emergency." Was it passive aggressive? Absolutely. But it got the message across.

I want to clarify that I'm not talking about the people-pleasing bug that's going around. I am talking about doing things we don't want to do because doing them would protect our image. **That's not people-pleasing; that's ego-pleasing.**

I'm talking about the things we do because the answer to the question "What would people say?" scares us so much that we don't even want to find out. It's a nasty demon called insecurity, also known as self-doubt.

It's a misconception that we need other people's approval or acceptance in order to love ourselves. In fact, if the only way we receive other people's approval is by doing something that is misaligned with our values, we won't love ourselves, we might end up hating ourselves.

Don't let fear of other people's disapproval deter you from staying on a path that **you** deem most important (be it your spiritual path, sobriety, your relationship, your career, retirement, your refusal to have children or to have a dozen). "To thine own self be true."

I think I've mentioned the following sentence in both of my other books and in every public talk: we are taught to be tolerant and accepting, but tolerance does not mean accepting what is harmful.

So, set some boundaries and stick to them. **If anything costs you your inner-peace, it's too expensive.**

"Courage is being yourself
in a world that tells you to be someone else."

Stubborn

"Stubborn" is defined as "having or showing persistent determination not to change one's attitude or position on something, especially in spite of good arguments or reasons to do so."

As soon as our mind is made up about something, it's difficult for us to change it because our egos don't particularly like admitting to being wrong about anything. In fact, even when proven wrong, many will strengthen their resolve rather than loosen their grip.

For many years, I insisted there was no reason to own anything other than shorts, T-shirts, and a pair of flip flops. This was true when I lived in Hawaii, but it hasn't been true since I moved back to the mainland, where it often gets much colder. Yet, silly as this may sound, I remained stubborn in my refusal to own warm clothes. Who was I hurting with my stubbornness to get winter gear? Myself. And why? Who was I protecting? My ego, of course. It makes no rational sense. And that's the problem with being stubborn, isn't it? It makes no rational sense.

The other day, I cut into an avocado that was brown and rancid on the inside. It was horrible! But what if that was someone's very first avocado experience? Would they decide that they didn't like avocados and never eat one again? Or strawberries, Brussel sprouts, sunflower seeds, or anything else with which they had one or two bad experiences?

We can spend our entire lives in a constant back-and-forth battle with the ego, or... what if we simply refrain from ever making our minds up about anything?

Just thinking about living that way sounds like a vacation! Never making our minds up about anything, staying open-minded, unrestricted, experimental, inquisitive, and willing to see everything from multiple angles.

I'm not talking about food anymore; we form rigid and uncompromising points of view about people, ideas, and beliefs, making it really difficult to change our minds in the future, even when we come across proof that we were previously wrong.

A friend of mine who still hates her ex-boyfriend, insists that people don't change. Since I personally know him, however, it's more accurate to say that her opinion of him is the only thing that hasn't changed; he is honestly a very different person than the man she met a dozen years ago.

Psychologically, we can rationalize whatever our minds conjure, so I never assume I'm right about anything. I try to remember to add the words "right now" to the end of every statement, such as "I don't like cauliflower (right now)," because who knows? Maybe it's really good with Buffalo Sauce? Which, by the way, I've tried it, and it's great (for right now). One day, I might not be able to stomach hot sauce anymore. It's counterproductive to be stubborn about anything. Those two simple words ("right now") keep the option open for us to change our minds and perspective at a later time.

To circle back to where the story started, I now have a fleece jacket, gloves, and a beanie. I can even camp in freezing temperatures without complaining. Okay... with LESS complaining. But, hey, it's a step in the right direction!

On what has your mind been firmly set before but changed over the years? Maybe even to the exact opposite? Think of foods, music, technology... you get the idea.

And to what opinions are you too firmly attached right now? What narrative can you benefit from changing to reduce rigidity and increase fluidity?

How are you creating obstacles that aren't even there? And more importantly, how can you remove them to liberate yourself from your own prison?

Are You Behind the Wheel?

I had a conversation with a tech support agent a couple of weeks ago on the phone. "Where are you located?" I asked. "Wisconsin," he answered. "Why are you there?" I inquired (a question I ask everyone regardless of where they live). "I was born and raised here," he explained, "and I guess I just stayed. My wife and I hate it though. We often talk about leaving, but now that you mention it, I don't know why we are still here."

Let's pretend our life is a road trip in the car. We start out as toddlers in the backseat, sometimes with siblings by our side, with our parents or guardians driving us around. They teach us what they know about the road, prepare us for possible hazards ahead, and point us in the direction they would like us to take on our own someday.

Around 18 years of age, we get out of our parents' car and into our own. We either take the on-ramp they have chosen for us to begin our journey, mimic their driving style, pace, and destination, or we peel out and speed in the opposite direction. Either way, we are now in control of our lives. We get to decide where to go and how fast to go there. More often than not, our lives are a complex combination of our own personal drive, parental influence, peer pressure, fears, compromise, circumstantial obstacles, a dash of luck, synchronicity and/or fate, depending on what you believe.

Decades later, some people are still on the same road their parents chose for them, while others have taken detours and dirt roads not listed on any map. Millions of people abandon their vehicles altogether, get on a bus or train instead, and just sit there, riding it to wherever it goes. They relinquish all control over the speed or destination of their lives, sometimes until the very last stop.

In many ways, that last choice is very appealing. Everything is predetermined, there are few surprises, and you can surf the web or watch TV while the conventional train chugs along.

In the old days, we only saw the people immediately around us, and everyone was on the same train or driving down the same road. But now, with social media, we regularly see pictures and videos that people share from all over the world. We are exposed to a whole new array of possibilities and realize how different life can be.

The moment we stop blaming other people for the way we choose to live, we discover more options available to us than we ever thought possible. I'm not suggesting there is a "right" or "wrong" way to go about it, only that it is imperative to remember two things: 1) At some point we made a choice about the life we currently have, and 2) We decide each day to either keep making that choice or to change direction. I've heard that we spend the first half of our lives blaming our parents for our situation, and the second half of our lives saying having kids is the reason we don't change our situation.

Even if we've been on the same bus for many years (or on a road that we wish was different), it's important not to feel stuck or victimized. We need to check-in with ourselves. Are we living the life we want? Is our job fulfilling us the way we thought it would? Is there anything on the back burner that needs to move to the front, or something on the front burner we can remove for good? When you ask yourself those questions and your answer is "I love my life and there is nowhere else I'd rather be," that's fantastic! Keep going. But if your answer motivates you to make a change, remember that just because you were born somewhere, for example, it doesn't mean you have to stay there. As the old saying goes, "If you don't like where you are, then move. You are not a tree."

By the time I got off the phone with the tech support agent, not only was my computer fixed, but he was excited to talk to his wife about moving. Replace your fear of the unknown with curiosity. Make the most out of life because it passes very quickly. **You** are behind the wheel… What are you waiting for?

> "The tragedy of life is not that it ends so soon,
> but that we wait so long to begin it."

Unhappily Ever After?

After having dinner at a couple's house the other night, I noticed their trash was piled in the corner of the kitchen **next** to the garbage can instead of **in** it. "We bought this high-tech bin a few years back," they explained, "then ran out of the special garbage bags for it about four months ago, and the manufacturer is still out of stock, so yeah... it's annoying."

"Why not get a new trash can that takes regular bags?" I asked.

"You'd think we would," they laughed, "but we've already spent so much money on this stupid thing," they said, pointing at the fancy, shiny, motion-activated, yet completely useless trash can in the corner, just sitting there mocking them.

I've also heard people complain about hanging out with certain friends because they don't have much to talk about or anything in common, so the conversation dies within a minute of meeting up.

"So why are you hanging out with them in the first place?" I'd ask.

"Well, we've known each other since elementary school," they'd reply, as if a history with someone implies there's also a future.

It seems we cling to our mistakes just because we've spent so much time, money, or energy, making them.

But I remember Steve (an attorney from one of the law firms where I used to work), storming out of his office one day, loudly announcing, "I am done! My dad was a lawyer, his father was a lawyer, and I was raised to believe that's exactly what I needed to be. But you know what? F*ck the years of law school and hundreds of thousands of dollars in student loans; I want to be a bartender! It's all I've ever wanted to be!" He put on his jacket, took the elevator down, and we never saw him again. Last I heard, he was happily tending bar somewhere in Seattle.

But Steve is the exception, not the rule. Most of us stay in miserable jobs, continue living in neighborhoods we dislike, and maintain dysfunctional relationships for decades, all because we think a change would require more energy than staying put.

A self-inquiry teacher named Papaji said, "What comes, let it come. What stays, let it stay. And what goes, let it go." We do well with what comes and what stays, but we fall short on letting things go.

What is it about release or surrender that scares us so much? Does it really stem from a core viewpoint of scarcity, or is our ego so afraid of being bruised that it regularly defends its bad decisions?

> "Don't cling to a mistake just because
> you spent a lot of time or money making it."

Relax? What's That?

When someone is stressed out, telling them to relax isn't very helpful. They might go as far as defend their stress as the appropriate response to their situation. And stress might be the habitual way they respond to most circumstances in life. I've heard it said that if the only tool you have is a hammer, everything starts to look like a nail. How we relate to the world, therefore, depends on our toolset. One person may have patience and inner peace at their disposal, while someone else may only have fear and frustration. Anger, for example, is like a jackhammer, which is helpful if your intention is to destroy something, but we need other tools if we want to build.

My friend Scott has little patience but a lot of money. When he has a problem, he tries to solve it by throwing money at it, but the underlying issue of his impatience never gets resolved. Watching Scott trying to figure out how to speed up time with money is like watching someone trying to quench their thirst with sand.

The problems in our lives are not frustrating situations and annoying people, the problem is that we keep getting annoyed and frustrated. Once we grow beyond annoyance and frustration, we just see them as people and situations because that's all they are. The goal isn't to create a bubble where nobody pushes our buttons; it's to get to a point where we don't have any buttons that can be pushed.

In the same way it's pointless to tell someone to calm down when they have no intention of calming down, the concept of peace is an absurd suggestion for someone invested in their fight. We can't force someone to suddenly see the world the way we do. So, don't exhaust yourself getting frustrated with people for not using tools they don't have. Just live your life; lead by example. There is no need to run around pointing your light at everybody. Simply shine like a lighthouse, and the ships that are ready to find their way out of the dark will gravitate towards you on their own when they are ready (and not a moment sooner).

Negativity Bias

It's been said that the truth can set us free, but from what? Does it liberate us from all the lies that hold us hostage?

I'm curious as to why we are so easily deceived in the first place, and whether it would make more sense for us to start taking everything with a grain of salt (not just what we hear from others, but the lies we tell ourselves as well).

The origin of "taking things with a grain of salt" (or with a bit of skepticism), has to do with making poison easier to swallow, whether that poison is actual venom or a potential lie.

My friend Eileen was diagnosed with cancer in the height of the COVID-19 pandemic. She asked that I move into her guesthouse and help out before, during, and after her scheduled surgery. Much to everyone's surprise, she tested positive for COVID two days before the operation, so the Department of Health (DOH) ordered both of us into strict quarantine, and the surgery was canceled.

As friends and members of her community started to panic, my impulse as caregiver was to take the test results with a grain of salt, get her re-tested as soon as possible, and calmly proceed from there.

It was interesting that even though the results of both the second and third tests that she took were negative, it was already too late. The original surgery slot was given to another patient, a neighbor spread distorted rumors about my friend infecting others with the Coronavirus, and the DOH refused to accept the negative test results as legit. They ordered a fourth test and sent the specimens from all the previous swabs to be re-tested by a state lab. And only when all of those tests came back negative, finally proving the first test simply showed an all-too-common false positive, Eileen was cleared for surgery.

Their caution was understandable, and I don't blame the DOH for wanting to be thorough. What I found surprising, however, was how quickly and easily everyone was willing to accept the first test results without question, yet how difficult it was to convince everyone that the opposite was actually true.

In psychology, that's referred to as Negativity Bias. It suggests that things of a more negative nature (such as unpleasant thoughts, social situations, or traumatic events), have a greater effect on us than positive or neutral events.

In case you're wondering, Eileen is doing well. Her surgery was quickly rescheduled, all the cancer was successfully removed, and we cruised through the recovery stage, grateful that all the delays just meant we got to spend more time together.

I'm not suggesting we always assume the best until the worst is proven true. I just think we need to get comfortable with the unknown and refrain from instinctively labeling situations as either "good" **or** "bad."

This experience reminded me of the ancient story about the old farmer whose horse ran away. When his neighbors heard the news, they came over and said, "Oh, such bad luck!" To which the farmer replied, "Maybe."

The next morning, the horse returned to the farm with three wild stallions. This time, the neighbors exclaimed, "Oh, how wonderful!" To which the old man said, "Maybe."

When the farmer's son tried to ride one of the untamed horses, he was thrown off and broke his leg. The neighbors said, "Oh, how unfortunate!" And again, the farmer replied, "Maybe."

The day after that, military officials came to the village to draft all the young men into a war from which very few soldiers had returned. Seeing that the boy's leg was broken, they left him behind.

The neighbors congratulated the farmer on how well things had turned out.

"Maybe," he said.

I love that story and try to live with that attitude about everything. As Gerry Spence brilliantly noted, "It is better to have a mind opened by wonder, than a mind closed by belief." And that's especially true if our beliefs are based on a negative bias.

So, loosen your grip on what you think you know is true, ask yourself why you believe what you do, and remember that the opposite of what is true for you is equally true for somebody else, somewhere else, depending on their time, place, or circumstance.

Perhaps enlightenment is not about some truth setting us free; maybe it's about recognizing which lies hold us hostage?

Maybe. I don't know.

> "The only thing I know for certain
> is that I don't know anything for certain,
> so I never argue with anyone about anything.
> I listen."

True Nature

I am often invited to speak at various churches, and I always ask, "How many of you believe in God?" Everyone raises their hands. Then I ask, "How many of you worry?" And most of them raise their hands again with a nervous chuckle, realizing what I'm up to.

"You either trust God or you worry; you can't do both!" I say, because worrying implies God has somehow dropped the ball or missed a memo.

One woman laughed and asked, "What if I'm a natural worrier?" And that question sparked a wonderful discussion.

When I was a teenager, my parents told everyone that I was a violent toddler and child. And whenever I got into trouble in school for what the teachers called "emotional outbursts," we blamed it on my "violent nature."

My friend Michelle is notoriously uncoordinated, falling off her bike, tripping on her shoes, always bleeding or limping for one reason or another, for which she blames her natural clumsiness. Her sister Ashley, on the other hand, is an amazing gymnast, often attributing her success to natural agility. People say it's in their nature to worry, my cousin refers to himself as a natural over-achiever, and I've spent my life making statements like, "Math doesn't naturally come to me like it does to many others."

But what if it's all a lie?

We tend to believe whatever we tell ourselves, so Michelle keeps getting hurt, Ashley just won another medal in gymnastics, I dismissed pursuing a career as an architect because it would have required too much math, and people who strongly believe in God continue to worry even though it directly contradicts having faith.

Turns out I'm not as "naturally violent" as my family thought I was (my outbursts were caused by learned behavior), and when I decided to go back to college after 18 years, I surprisingly aced all of my math classes. This empowered me to tackle other challenges that I believed I was predestined to fail.

What do you believe is your true nature? Is it possible you've been wrong all along?

We can overcome much more than we ever thought was possible by first believing that we can (individually and collectively). All we need is a little trust that everything naturally balances out (it always has, even if it rarely happens the way we think it should, and hardly ever as quickly as we would like). Our resistance is the only thing that's "unnatural," but it's just learned behavior that we can unlearn.

What if our true nature is the same as that of nature itself: to adapt? And what if all our anguish is a result of our refusal to do just that?

Our Buddha-nature is to live in harmony with all that is. So, the question is, are you being the Buddha you were born to be, or are you fighting nature?

"The best remedy for those who are afraid, lonely, or unhappy,
is to go outside, somewhere where they can be quiet,
alone with the heavens, nature, and God.
Because only then does one feel that everything is as it should be,
and that God wishes to see people happy,
amidst the simple beauty of nature.
I firmly believe that nature brings solace in all troubles."
—Anne Frank

Sharp Edges

A friend once told me, "Everything I ever let go of had claw marks in it," and I laughed because I can relate. We tend to cling to everything with a firm grip, whether it's a strong opinion, an unwavering belief that we are right, a specific way to do something, or an outright refusal to try something new. When Bruce Lee said, "Be water, my friend," it was because that which is rigid, breaks.

Many teachers over the years have pointed out my "on/off button," as they called it, and urged me to install a dimmer switch, so to speak. That's because I tend to be all-in with something or not in at all (Go Big or Go Home... you get the idea).

I used to confuse moderation with mediocrity until I learned the difference. What I thought was my conviction and dedication, others saw as me being extremely hardcore, brutal, intense, and even insensitive (specifically when I leaned too heavily on logic and rationale, completely dismissive of the sentimental or emotional). People thought I was heartless, cold, and distant.

Unfortunately, we usually can't see our own sharp edges until we hurt ourselves or others. Recently, a close friend chose to shine a light on one of my sharp edges, and she helped me better understand the problem. "It's great that you have boundaries," she said, "but is the barbed wire and electric fence around them really necessary?"

It blew my mind. I had always considered my boundaries to be healthy (and they arguably are), but how I respond to people who test those boundaries can most definitely use a gentler approach than definitively shutting them out.

Sadly, gentleness is not a skill I had ever learned, and my existing pattern was so deeply embedded, I don't even realize when I'm being rigid until it's too late.

Luckily, my friend was not only reflective and understanding of my own sharp edges, she also confessed to being rigid in her own ways. If someone else loads the dishwasher, she takes out all the dirty dishes and reloads them because she likes it done a certain way. She is anxious about showing up late to anything, and she immediately thinks less of people who use profanity.

She told me her daughter's rigidity shows up in how harshly she judges the way people look (and therefore herself), and her son is unyielding and stubborn about the things he refuses to do, such as camping, going a day without coffee, or eating alone at a restaurant on a Friday night (which he insists is strictly for "Date Night!").

When I was new to meditation, I put on a very serious face and told the Zen teacher that my mantra was "Like a deeply-rooted tree I shall remain."

He just laughed and said, "Make sure it's one of those palm trees that can sway in the wind!"

He didn't even know the meaning of my birth name (Tomer) is literally Palm Tree, and my original last name (Gal) means Ocean Wave. Yup, my parents named me "Palm Tree, Ocean Wave," and my life's journey has been to sway in the wind and go with the flow.

My intention is to transition from rigidity to being gentler with myself and with others. What I have found is that when I intentionally apply gentleness in one area of my life, it makes it possible for me to be gentler in other areas as well.

For example, I've been on a plant-based diet for many years, so none of my dishes or utensils at home have ever touched meat, dairy or eggs. But when friends invite me over for dinner and go out of their way to grill vegetables for me, I know their pan was used to grill a steak the night before, but I say "Thank you," and I enjoy the meal with tremendous gratitude for their generosity. I still won't eat animals, of course, and I remain rooted in my values, but this tree can now sway in the wind.

As I continue the practice of letting go, I am a better friend to people I meet today than I have been to those I've known for the past 40+ years.

This may be a strange example of loosening my grip, but silence is my favorite sound. So, in the old days, whenever I went on long road trips in the car with friends, we either rode in complete silence, or we only listened to the music **I** chose (sounds like a whole lot of fun, doesn't it?!)

On a recent car ride with a friend, however, I consciously decided ahead of time to completely let go of any attempt to control the stereo. We listened to whatever she wanted to play on the radio, because I essentially decided that our friendship was more important than my rigidity or being in control. I not only survived the trip, we ended up having a great time!

We all have sharp edges and rigidity about certain things, and we may even feel justified about them. But what happens when our rigidity works against us, and we refuse to bend? That which is rigid breaks, remember?

Can you think of any of your own sharp edges that hurt you and the people around you?

Our rigidity often works against us, and if we have our claws so deeply embedded in the way we were, we get in the way of who we might become.

So, practice letting go of one stubborn opinion at a time; try things you swore you never would; and learn to listen to others without interrupting them (even if they disagree with what you believe).

> "You can't reach for anything new
> if your hands are still full
> of yesterday's junk."
> — Louise Smith

The Message is Love

Religion is a collection of beliefs and philosophies, and I've always had my own, but it wasn't organized nor affiliated with any existing school of thought.

Through personal experiences, observation, trial and error, I have developed some habits that one could presume were based on religion (but were not): I don't drink, smoke, eat meat, consume stimulants, or have casual sex, for example. Instead, I spend a lot of time in nature or meditating, and I believe we are here to learn to be completely selfless. I've never had a name for it, I just called it Timberism.

The first time I heard the Dalai Lama speak, he talked about self-control, determination, and freedom from anger, which were the same concepts I had tattooed on my chest three years prior. He said, "kindness is my religion," and I think that's as good a label as any.

When my friend met her favorite author, she was disappointed to discover he wasn't the sage she had projected him to be. It's important to focus on the message, not the messenger. The message is always fundamentally the same—the core of the message is love.

When somebody else's story resonates with us, we realize we are not alone. That realization is an important step in breaking down our delusions of grandeur, bringing us closer together. After all, nothing makes us feel more alone than our secrets.

"Enlightened" is not something you become one day, it's something to continually cultivate. The dictionary defines enlightenment as "having or showing a rational, modern, and well-informed outlook exhibited by our behavior." We can all do that, right?

The best way to honor our teachers is to do as they have done. We are all messengers, what message are you spreading?

Effort

We want everything in life to be easy, comfortable, and pleasant. It sounds harmless and innocent, but life has its difficult moments, and while there is no way around them, there is a way through.

The problem with wanting things to always be easy is that it stops us from intentionally pursuing challenging situations, which is where true growth happens.

We can learn more from trying and failing than we ever could from not trying at all. That's because life experiences can humble us, open our hearts, and fill us with gratitude.

Constantly choosing the path of least resistance takes us further from where we ultimately want to be (physically, mentally, spiritually, and emotionally). We achieve a sense of accomplishment from running a marathon, for example, not from winning it. Millions of people sign up to run specifically because triumph comes from effort; THAT is the achievement.

This isn't about actually running 26.2 miles; I'm talking about not whining about results we don't get from effort we refuse to make.

People often complain about things they actually **can** change. It's important to acknowledge the difference between "difficult" and "impossible." We are too quick to give up when things seem hard.

Take something as simple as removing a screw from a piece of wood. It is possible but impractical to remove the screw with a butter knife. It's easier with an actual screwdriver, and it's a breeze with a power drill. Spiritual practice is about developing new tools to get the screw unstuck (whether that means patiently using a butter knife to remove it ever-so-slowly and with much effort, or diligently working for many years to get that power drill). Any progress is better than none.

Determination, purpose, and intention propel us forward in life. Buddhism is the gentle vehicle that simultaneously acknowledges we are already perfect the way we are, then showing us how to improve.

There is no guilt, shame, or regrets. There are only experiments and lessons. That's why Zen practice is not about turning away from painful thoughts or feelings; it's about facing them until they are not so scary anymore.

So, don't avoid challenges; get curious about them. Challenges are there to challenge you, after all, not to stop you in your tracks.

We all have moments of feeling "stuck" (whether it's in our way of thinking or our way of being). It's why I frequently challenge myself to attempt what I have previously deemed too uncomfortable or difficult to even try (such uphill challenges over the years have included learning to be vulnerable and transparent, understanding opposing beliefs, finishing projects that I had started but neglected for far too long, climbing mountains, or walking around the block when it's the last thing I want to do). Whatever feels uncomfortable for you, START there, don't stop there! Unscrew yourself, so to speak, and you'll be glad you did.

To make any progress on the path, we need to get out of our own way. The armor I wore in the past to protect myself in abusive situations, and the walls I had built around me when I was younger in order to feel safe, would actually work against me today if I don't let them go.

There is a lot here to unpack, so start by questioning whether what you've deemed "insurmountable" is really just difficult. Sometimes, all you need is some confidence and effort to put one foot in front of the other.

To quote the movie *Shawshank Redemption*, "Get busy living, or get busy dying."

Are You Ready?

My former roommate had a big hiking trip planned, so she trained for it daily to make the experience less difficult. Another friend was looking for a new job, so he regularly attended mock interviews in preparation for the real thing. Athletes train, authors write rough drafts, pilots go through flight simulations, and I constantly practice letting go of everything I fear losing, which makes life's challenges less of a struggle.

I have even imagined a doctor telling me I have cancer, for example (which may or may not happen), just as I have mentally prepared myself for the inevitable news of my father's death. It may sound like I'm torturing myself, but going through the motions in meditation is like training; I feel ready. As Thich Nhat Hanh said, "When you learn **how** to suffer, you suffer much less."

A few years ago, I took inventory of everything in my life to which I had grown attached, and then I donated all of it (outfits that I liked, souvenirs from various trips, my favorite books, and all of my music). My friends didn't understand why I felt so liberated, so when I heard Tyler Durden say, "The things you own end up owning you," I made everyone watch *Fight Club*. (I don't actually recommend you watch the movie; it is extremely graphic and violent, so maybe read the book instead?)

Nothing I currently own holds any sentimental value, so if my home were to catch on fire, there is nothing in it I would try to save.

We put a lot of energy into our precious possessions, which explains why they have so much power over us. And by getting rid of tangible items, we also get rid of vanity, greed, and fear. I'm not suggesting you sell everything you own, but freedom from suffering can be attained by eliminating the very causes of it: desire and attachment.

When you regularly practice walking towards what makes you uncomfortable, the discomfort subsides. And when you start looking at someone you despise as a human being who is full of anguish, pain, fear, and insecurities, your hatred transforms into compassion. It sounds counterintuitive to do exactly the opposite of what you feel like doing, but as the old saying goes, "The cave you fear to enter holds the treasure you seek." In this case, the treasure is freedom from suffering. The question is, do you want it badly enough to do whatever it takes, including staying connected to everything yet attached to nothing?

The same way professionals in every field hone their skills through practice, let's become professionals at fully living by mentally readying ourselves to calmly face whatever comes next (prepared to observe and maybe respond, but never react).

What are you most attached to? It may be an outcome, a ritual, a piece of art, your routine, or your youthful skin.

Can you practice letting it go? Not because there is anything inherently wrong with it, but because attachment to it has a lot of power over you. You can get that power back through practice.

I'd read somewhere that if a monkey hoarded more bananas than he could eat while letting other monkeys starve, scientists would study that monkey to figure out what is wrong with him. But when humans do it, we put them on the cover of *Forbes* and *Fortune* magazines.

If we raise our standard of living, we need to raise our standard of giving. It's that simple.

> "When you have more than you need,
> build a longer dining table,
> not a taller fence."

Privilege

What is privilege? What is it not? Who has it? And what can we do with it?

Privilege is an advantage available to a particular person or group, and it is often unearned.

In the United States, despite the supposed separation of Church and State, school holidays and paid time off work was (and still is), scheduled around Christian holidays. That is Christian privilege.

Since I was born Jewish, however, I had to either ask for special treatment, or still go to school and work because the Jewish calendar is not recognized here. Lacking Christian privilege was perhaps my first face-to-face confrontation with an uphill climb I have inherited through no fault of my own, while the majority enjoyed unchallenged time off with their families.

The State of California recognizes Indigenous Peoples' Day (while many other States in the U.S. still celebrate Columbus Day), and nowhere but in the State of Hawaii does anyone know about, let alone observe, King Kamehameha or Prince Kuhio Day. When I was younger, I thought privilege was simply a matter of majority rules, but there are more women than men, yet it's still considered "a man's world."

I am privileged in that I am currently able-bodied. I didn't earn my privilege, and I can't get rid of it, but it's important to acknowledge it, and then to use it to help those who aren't equally represented.

When someone tells you to "check your privilege," the suggestion is that you recognize the advantageous position you are in. Even being attractive according to cultural standards is a privilege with its own perks and benefits (or so I hear), so this chapter is truly about privilege without any political agenda between the lines.

Some male actors are now refusing to accept roles in movies where their female co-stars are paid less than they are. It's a step in the right direction, requiring privileged men to be allies for women. Allies are necessary for evolution and in every revolution.

People get very defensive when others point out their privilege, but there is no need to be. I am fully aware that I am privileged because I can pass for white and I identify as cis-male. Those are two unearned advantages.

However, someone tried to shame me online for being privileged because I don't have any children or a family to support, but that's not privilege, that's a choice. Luckily, someone who **is** a parent commented that parents are actually the privileged ones because they get to raise children while so many people literally cannot.

Another example of when we witness the destructive force of privilege is when a person looks at someone else's struggle and says, "Well, that's not my problem!"

Rather than being the voice for those who aren't heard, this attitude increases the distance between us.

Privilege is not something for others to use against us, it's something we must all understand and use as a tool to create the balance we seek. From a Buddhist perspective, just being born is a privilege. Life is a gift to which the only appropriate response is "Thank you."

Let's use our personal advantages to help others advance. Equal rights for others does not mean fewer rights for you... it's not cake!

So, contemplate the benefits you enjoy, whether you've earned them or not, and use that privilege to help others.

Embracing our interconnectedness is what Buddhism is all about. It's a practice we can all master.

In fact, it's a privilege to have been exposed to the teachings in the first place.

Generosity

When I asked people online what comes to mind when they think of generosity, thousands responded, and most referenced things like generous donations, a generous job offer, or leaving a generous tip at a restaurant. All the answers were money-related, which is why most people don't consider themselves generous (having never given a large sum of money to a non-profit organization, or sponsored the arts in their town with annual contributions).

This reminds me of a roadblock I encountered when I initially tried to raise funds for our Books-to-Prisons Program a few years ago. I posted a copy of the $20,000 invoice I got to print the books in paperback (because prisons don't allow hardcovers). A week into our campaign, only three people donated (a hundred dollars each), which was generous, but nowhere near enough to meet our goal. Everyone else saw that invoice and thought, "Well, I can't pay for that, so don't look at me." I decided to change my strategy, removed the invoice, and simply asked that people donate just one dollar each. We not only reached our goal, but nearly 20,000 people had the opportunity to be generous by a whole new definition: not by donating a thousand dollars, but with just a buck. I think it was a greater victory than getting 10 people to donate $2,000. It was empowering and extremely rewarding for everyone involved. We underestimate our ability to be generous.

And generosity doesn't have to be monetary. We can all be generous with our time, skills, talent, and even space. As you may know, whenever I travel on a book tour (even when I was on the road for three consecutive years across the U.S., UK, and Australia), I never stay in hotels. People offer me their couch or a guest bedroom for a night or two, which is how I continue being generous with my time (never charging a speaking fee and making the events free for all).

Now, proceeds from book sales support our Books-to-Prisons Programs, so I no longer need to run fundraisers. We are not talking about one random act of kindness anymore; we are talking about generosity as a sustainable business model. It's possible!

We are all familiar with generous giving, but a friend recently introduced me to the concept of generously receiving. What does that even mean? Well, look at the 20,000 people who donated one dollar to help us reach our fundraising goal, or all the people who support the *Buddhist Boot Camp Podcast* on *Patreon* so that the podcast doesn't need to be sponsored by commercials for car insurance or a mattress-in-a-box. The podcast isn't mine; it's ours.

When *Buddhist Boot Camp* was first incorporated in Oregon a few years ago, a local attorney loved my vision statement so much that she offered her services for free. There's an old man who attends my monthly discussion circles in California who always brings fresh fruit from his yard. Generosity has many faces.

If you have good eyesight, you can read to the blind. If you have a car, you can offer rides to the elderly in your community so they can get to the grocery store and back. Couchsurfing was founded years ago on the simple idea that almost everyone has a couch that they can offer to someone traveling the world on a budget and needing a place to sleep for a night or two. I've had wonderful experiences as both a guest and a host to couchsurfers from all over the world. Recently, I hosted a couchsurfer who took a year and a half off from work to ride a bicycle from South America all the way to Canada. When we hosted him, he was already a year and three months into his journey, having clocked more than 10,000 miles on his bike. He needed a place to stay for the night, a warm shower, and a place to do his laundry. Why in the world would we say, "No," to him?

What I'm saying is that we need to change the way we think of generosity as strictly financial. There are numerous ways in which we can enrich the lives of others, which automatically enriches our own lives as well.

As Saint Francis of Assisi said, "It's in giving that we receive."

The People Upstairs

I've never been as upset with someone I've never actually met as I was with whoever was living upstairs from where I was dogsitting for a friend. Every sliding door in the unit upstairs sounded like a train going through my friend's apartment below, and every footstep above shook the picture frames on the walls next to me. I swear it once even sounded like they were bowling in the living room. On my third day there, construction started on their bathroom renovation. I was absolutely exhausted, violently furious, and, as my friend says, "The streets of my mind were not safe for anyone."

I couldn't get any work done during the day, and I didn't get any sleep at night because I couldn't stop thinking about how inconsiderate it was for the people upstairs to do whatever they wanted with no regard for how their decisions negatively impacted others. Suddenly, any thought about "the people upstairs" took on a whole new meaning; it wasn't just the neighbors above me, it became a reference to the people "at the top" who pass laws that affect everyone below. In business-speak, it's a reference to upper management making decisions that affect every employee, and in politics, it's the Supreme Court impacting local regulations. "The people upstairs" (and I'm no longer talking about the neighbors above me), are the ones who get to decide what noise is considered a nuisance and what is not. Can they tell people not to run the dishwasher after 9pm because it sounds like a airplane taking off in the apartment below, or would that restriction infringe on the tenants' rights to do whatever they want whenever they want to do it?

Keep in mind, my friend has been paying thousands of dollars each month for the past three years to live in an apartment that he absolutely loves (completely unbothered by the same noise that nearly caused me to lose my mind). Does that mean it's perfectly okay for the people upstairs to be completely inconsiderate of how their choices affect others? That's a tough question to answer; whom do we ask?

Every spiritual teacher I've ever had has held both of my hands in theirs at one point, looked me in the eyes, and said, "Oh Timber, you are such an idealist." And it's true. I'm not suggesting tenants shouldn't be allowed to renovate their bathrooms, but it would've been nice to receive notice in advance so that everyone in the building could plan accordingly. Some buildings enforce such requirements, but others do not. If my friend wanted to, he could afford to move somewhere else, but that's a luxury many don't have.

There are people in apartments, cities, states, or countries where decisions made by "the people upstairs" impact their everyday lives. I recall my visit to the Philippines, for example, where divorce isn't an option because "the people upstairs" are against it. Is that absurd, or is it absurd that more than half of marriages in the U.S. end in divorce? I don't know.

We can't all live on the top floor, and we can't all stay happily married 'til death do us part. So, we keep changing "the people upstairs," who keep switching the rules that dictate what is allowed and what is forbidden. Perhaps we'll keep dancing that way until the end of time. Every community that has attempted to implement one rigid set of rules to apply to everyone has eventually deteriorated because it became exclusive instead of inclusive. This explains why Christianity now has more than 45,000 denominations around the world. There is no "one size fits all."

The problem at my friend's apartment wasn't the poor construction of the building, nor the mindlessness of the people upstairs, maybe the problem was that I kept trying to make my friend's place what it wasn't: a quiet sanctuary. If this helps one person become more mindful of others, then I consider it a win (whether they literally live upstairs from someone or they pass laws that affect everyone).

Don't get me wrong, the apartment has its redeeming qualities, but silence wasn't one of them. Every place has redeeming qualities, and it's up to us to keep that in mind. As Confucius said, "Everything has beauty, but not everyone sees it."

Never Broken

When I speak at various congregations, there are always songs before and after my talk. At one of those services, a woman sang about being like one of those Japanese bowls, where the breaks are mended by filling the cracks with gold. Rather than hiding the imperfections, they are made to shine. All the jagged lines make them more beautiful and valuable. If we don't hide the places where we have broken, everyone will see we are not who we used to be.

After an abusive upbringing, a few suicide attempts, and many years of therapy, I spoke to Reverend Sky in Hawaii about my childhood, and he stopped me mid-sentence to point out that my narrative was still that of a victim. I was identifying with that broken, little boy, rather than leaving him in the past. He gently pointed out that moving on from the past is not the same as burying it. We can extract strength from those experiences, or as Maya Angelou beautifully said, "I can be changed by what happened in my life, but I refuse to be reduced by it."

So, like those Japanese bowls, I no longer hide my past with shame, guilt, anger, resentment, or regret. I openly share what I've been through, and many readers have confirmed that they've had similar difficulties in their own lives. There is no reason for any of us to feel ashamed of where we have cracked in the past. We are still here. And as Jewel shared in her memoir entitled *Never Broken,* "We can rise from the screaming blood of our losses, of extreme pain, physical, debilitating emotion, psychological neglect, and apathy, and not merely survive, but thrive. But believing we are broken is the same as being broken."

I have never met a strong person with an easy past, so I am grateful for everything that shaped me; it's the gold that shines through.

> "Don't just go through life,
> grow through life."

Outrospection

It's good to balance introspection with outrospection. As a kid, I used to spend hours alone in my room. When I misbehaved, my parents couldn't punish me by yelling, "Go to your room," because that's where I always wanted to be. Instead, they locked me out of the house and said, "Go play outside like a normal kid. Make some friends!"

I am not condoning this parenting method, but in hindsight, it probably did me some good. This was years before we had terms for introverts or kids on the autism spectrum. Children were either considered well-adjusted if they conformed and behaved like everyone else, or they were considered outcasts.

The only place I fit in with others was in after-school programs to learn robotics. That's where I made a couple of friends who mostly kept to themselves as well. Even though alone-time is healthy, so were the hours I was forced to socialize with others.

Just as I was entering my teens, my family moved from a small town in Israel to California. The high school I attended in San Francisco had more students in it than the population of the town where I grew up, and a whole lot more diversity. I was suddenly surrounded by Asians, Blacks, and Latinos. It was a culture shock. Had I not been forced to socialize as a young kid, I might have gone into actual shock or withdrawn even more than usual.

I'm not saying I was well-adjusted (I'm still not), but I managed to quickly learn English, make some friends, and stay curious about everyone's culture, religion, and ethnic background. Nothing and no one resembled anything to which I had previously been exposed, so I asked a lot of questions.

Long before the Internet was born, even before computers had windows or mice, I joined what was called SF-Net. It was a network of computers in coffee shops around the San Francisco Bay Area with coin-operated dial-up modems, offering a chat room of sorts for up to 30 people at a time, either dialing-in from their homes or from other coffee shops in the area. We called ourselves "Netters," and we organized "net-gets" (such as bonfires on the beach or meetups at bars on Haight and Ashbury back when nobody checked your ID to get in).

I met people from all walks of life, including college students, adults, and some kids my own age who were homeless by choice because the streets were safer than the broken homes from which they escaped.

Coming from a small town, I recall being blown away the first time I saw someone with blue hair and facial piercings, but nothing shocked me after a couple of weeks on the streets of Berkeley in the 90s. I lost the knee-jerk judgment that my parents had (and attempted to instill in me) about other races, religions, the unsheltered, and the misunderstood. I firmly believe that visibility leads to acceptance.

Consider what it must have been like for people to see interracial or same-sex couples holding hands a few decades ago (or even recently in some parts of the world). It was a shock the first time, but it lessens the more frequently people are exposed to it. Again, visibility leads to acceptance.

Exposure opens our eyes first, our minds second, and our hearts third. The key to empathy and compassion, therefore, is connection; not just seeing punk rockers on TV, but having coffee with them on a Thursday night.

In the best way possible, the exposure I had in California's Bay Area as a teenager "forced me" to grow up in much the same way I was forced out of the house when I was younger. The only difference is that I resisted it less (and it has forever changed me). Our comfort zone is expandable.

Generally speaking, residents of major metropolitan cities are exposed to diverse cultures, beliefs, and backgrounds on a daily basis, so they tend to be more open-minded than people who never leave rural areas. That absence of exposure and connection leads to people who are different being judged as "freaks." But we can't expect the so-called "freaks" to move to rural areas in order to open people's eyes, minds, and hearts; it's up to each one of us (regardless of where we live), to stop thinking of anyone as "other," and to choose curiosity over judgment.

Whenever I'm being judgmental of others, the problem is me.

I would go as far as to say that it's only through outrospection that introspection is even possible. We wouldn't even know that we were being judgmental if our rigid boundaries weren't challenged, and we can't heal what we refuse to confront.

It's not somebody else's job to explain themselves to me; it's up to me to do the work, to look outside myself, and to understand the bigger picture where there is room for everybody.

I am another you, and you are another me.

"We are here to awaken
from our illusion of separateness."
—Thich Nhat Hanh

Incentive

There is incentive behind everything we do. We exercise to stay healthy, save money so we can go on vacation, and brush our teeth to avoid cavities. So, what's the incentive behind meditation? This chapter is my effort to explain how meditation helps me.

Let's say you decide to give meditation a try. You don't need to spend thousands of dollars on meditation retreats, and you don't need to fly to Nepal to sit in a cave (unless that's your thing). You can simply sit in a chair or on the floor, and don't move for a set period of time. If you have an itch, don't scratch it. If your foot falls asleep, don't change positions. If your mind starts making up stories about a spider crawling on your head, let it (without giving into the fear).

This meditative practice of sitting and observing our urges without reacting to them is extraordinarily powerful. It's an exercise in not allowing our thoughts to control our impulses. This impacts our daily interactions in many ways: if someone does something annoying, for example, you can choose not to get annoyed (just like you chose not to scratch that itch while you were sitting). If you find yourself in a frustrating situation, you don't lose your temper (just like you didn't move when your foot fell asleep during meditation). And when you get anxious about the future, you know the anxiety will subside through patience (just like when your mind created the story about a spider crawling on your head and you waited for it to pass because you knew it wasn't true).

Sitting still doesn't mean resisting the mind's tendency to wander. Sitting is a disciplined practice of observing the mind to better understand how it works.

Even though sitting doesn't immediately change your life (just like one visit to the gym doesn't make you lose weight), if you commit to sitting regularly, you will eventually find yourself consciously choosing not to stress in the middle of stressful situations, and remaining calm even when surrounded by annoying people.

Most of us spend our lives trying to avoid those who push our buttons, and we often get mad at them when they do. But the incentive of mindfulness practice is to get to a place where we no longer have any buttons that can be pushed.

Sit in a chair or on the floor, set a timer for a few minutes, close your eyes, and don't move until the time is up. Your mind will wander, let it. You'll be tempted to open your eyes, don't. You will be convinced that you have to itch your arm or leg, but notice what happens when you don't. Just sit there. Don't shift in your seat or stretch; you can do that later. The benefit of acknowledging each impulse but not reacting to it will not be apparent while you are sitting, but the practice will prove useful later in the day when you notice an impulse to lash out, for example, but you hold yourself back. The rewards from this practice benefit you and everyone around you. When the timer is up, that's when you can rub your foot, scratch that itch, or stretch. It's a small but powerful exercise in patience, self-control, and determination. Do it daily.

As I often say,

"Mindfulness doesn't make other people less irritating,
it makes us less irritable."

The Gift of Time

Almost every spiritual tradition teaches us the importance of practicing gratitude. We know grateful people are happy people, yet many of us don't fully appreciate the roof over our heads or food in our stomachs, probably because we've never had to go without.

There's a Zen story about a student who told his teacher that focusing on the breath during meditation was boring. So, the teacher submerged the student's head under water until the student kicked and struggled to come up for air, at which point the master released his grip, looked the student in the eye, and asked, "Do you still think the breath is boring?"

Can we train ourselves and others to appreciate each and every little thing in life without having to go without it for a while? It would take shifting our perspectives from feeling entitled to the time we have on this earth to seeing time as a gift from a mysterious stranger.

The reason I suggest considering our time a "gift" is because then we wouldn't need to learn anything new to practice gratitude; we are already familiar with feeling thankful when someone gives us a present. But what happens when you receive a gift you don't particularly like? Or, better yet, how would you respond if your car breaks down during a very difficult time in your life (financially and otherwise), leaving you with no way to get to work, and someone offers you a free bicycle so you don't lose your job? Would you be grateful? What if it's not a brand-new bike? What if it's old and rusty without any gears? Would you turn down this generous offer because it isn't up to your standards, or would you be extremely grateful for the possibilities this less-than-ideal solution represents?

Now think of the lifetime we are each given. It is often painful, challenging, and uncomfortable, but it's free time nonetheless. If we look at everything as a gift, then a rusty bike and a new car are equally valuable.

Just think about that word "valuable" in this context. It means you can find value in your ability to move forward—whether it's by bus, a skateboard, or your own two feet if you are fortunate enough to have them (and skillful enough to appreciate them). This practice goes beyond seeing the glass as half full or half empty, it's about being grateful to have a glass in the first place.

The antidote to our sense of entitlement is gratitude, and I truly believe we can learn to appreciate the difficult times in our lives just as much as the smooth sailing. We don't need a near-death experience to appreciate our lives, do we?

Your challenge for today is to not only think of everything for which you are grateful, but to contemplate WHY you are grateful for it, and how it affects your life.

Marinate in that feeling of gratitude until it comes out your pores in the form of a smile, kindness, and generosity.

This isn't my usual invitation to examine how we create our own suffering. It is a reminder to be thankful for the good, the bad, and the most horrific times in our lives, because we cannot love ourselves if we still hate or resent the experiences that shaped us. Yes, all of them.

> "Thankfulness is the beginning of gratitude.
> Gratitude is the completion of thankfulness.
> Thankfulness may consist merely of words.
> Gratitude is shown in acts."
> — Henri Frederic Amiel

Altruism

It's been said that the meaning of life is to give life meaning (to search for, find, and be motivated by a sense of purpose or a mission). The mission doesn't have to be grand or philanthropic entrepreneurship, running an orphanage, or saving lives. It can be whatever fuels you to get out of bed each morning. For some people, raising children is the ultimate calling, while for others, the mission relates to their vocation, artistic expression, or a meaningful objective of progress (be it environmental, humanitarian, or spiritual).

Regardless of the path we choose, many people still feel "empty" despite having money in the bank, a big house, and the latest iPhone. That's because those things don't give our life **meaning**. Altruism (not consumerism) is the path to true fulfillment. I was taught that when your life lacks meaning, you distract yourself with pleasure.

That being said, we **are** all consumers, so I'm not suggesting we start leading austere, ascetic lives. I do believe, however, that making mindful purchase decisions has a meaningful impact, not just on the world outside of us, but also within.

An altruistic lifestyle is not just for billionaires, it's available to everyone who wants to avoid feeling "empty" inside.

The key is to practice discernment at every turn. Whenever I'm tempted to buy something, I first ask myself why I want to buy it. If I think it will "make me happy," then I leave it in the store because I already know material things only momentarily boost my mood, they are not an investment in my overall well-being. Healthy food, on the other hand, or supporting organizations that are doing incredible work in the world, can lead to true fulfillment.

So, when I need to buy something useful, I contemplate **where** to buy it, and the decision of which retailer I want to support is where altruism comes in. We vote with our wallets; we decide which businesses get to stay in business and which do not. Choose wisely.

Self-Worth

From a very young age, many of us have been told that we need to prove our worth. We started by seeking praise from our parents, teachers, preachers, and peers, then maybe worked hard to be deemed good enough to get into college. Dating is a constant attempt to feel worthy of love, and climbing the corporate ladder is about being recognized as valuable enough for a promotion. We grew up believing there is a void within us that can only be filled by others, and the social media platform was built to temporarily fill that void each time someone "likes" our posts.

Raised with organized religion, many believe they were born sinners, and the ultimate reveal determines whether they are worthy enough to get into heaven.

According to Buddhism, however, we are not born sinners; we are actually all born with Buddha-nature and the ability to awaken from any illusion of unworthiness. The Buddhist concept of hell is not a destination we might reach after we die; it's what we experience while we are alive until we learn to overcome greed, hatred, and ignorance. Salvation, therefore, is gained by learning to live in peace with ourselves and others.

While organized religion asks us to accept what it preaches as the truth (discouraging questions and doubt), spirituality does the exact opposite: it tells us NOT to accept any truth without first questioning it (even if it's given to us by someone of great stature). We are urged to investigate everything we are told the way a jeweler examines gold for authenticity before accepting it as real.

We were raised on a system of hierarchy, even within our families, where we are compared to our cousins who are doing so well, or we are told to be more like our siblings. Our sense of worth is not a contest. I don't even think our job titles give us value; we add value to the world by doing our jobs with integrity (whether we are performing brain surgery or washing dishes). If our job is done with integrity, it can be fulfilling and altruistic. But without integrity, even the most honorable position loses its merit.

I have watched Buddhist priests treat people around them with hostility, impatience, and disregard, and I have seen heads of non-profit organizations driven by their egos instead of an unwavering dedication to their cause. We don't all need to be the Dalai Lama's personal assistant to bring a sense of fulfillment or purpose to our lives. The world requires that each of us do our part to make it function, and no gear or tooth in this big ol' machine is less or more valuable than another. A car's engine isn't more important than its tires; we need both for the car to move.

Without dismissing brain surgeons, I'm extending a deep bow of gratitude to those of us who wash and sanitize the surgical tools, mop the floor in the hospital room, or drive the ambulance. Dare I say, it's the people behind the scenes, the unsung heroes, invisible contributors, anonymous donors, and silent do-gooders, who inspire me more than those in the headlines.

Whatever you do in the world, you are making a difference that many people appreciate. If they never express their gratitude, that's a failure on their part. Many of us are grateful for construction workers, customer service personnel, teachers, bank tellers, flight attendants, custodians, ministers, programmers, bookkeepers, servers, mechanics, grocery store clerks, retail workers, miners, farmers, pilots, cashiers, plumbers, bus drivers, house cleaners, accountants, engineers, nurses, search-and-rescue personnel, lawyers, politicians, strippers, chefs, midwives, secretaries, actors, judges, artists, librarians, stay-at-home parents, and yes, Buddhist priests and surgeons too.

We all serve a purpose. And even though some of us have lost our sense of fulfillment, we can get it back if we bring a renewed awareness of our interconnectedness and the intention to heal into everything we do.

Ask yourself when you started believing that you must prove your worth to someone other than yourself in order to have value.

Determine what integrity looks like for you.

By what set of guiding principles do you aspire to live?

And, at the end of each day, acknowledge that if you've lived in line with your values, then you can be at peace with yourself. Don't measure how much good you do in the world compared to someone else. Simply focus on doing less harm, and you would immediately be part of the solution simply by not being part of the pollution.

Some people are just starting on their spiritual journey, and others have been up and down these trails for many years. Nobody has ever reached a point where the road ends because it's not a journey to a destination; we evolve to a transformation.

So, it doesn't matter for how long you've been on the path or from which direction you came, we are all kindred spirits.

Unpack some of the ideas you started believing while you were growing up, and see if they are beneficial or detrimental to your well-being today.

"It is the mark of an educated mind
to entertain a thought without necessarily accepting it."
— Aristotle

Trust Yourself

My friend Stacy and I were on a road trip in the car. A song came on the radio, and she said, "Ooh, I like this." We bopped our heads to the beat, and she asked, "Who's the artist?" As soon as I told her who it was, she said, "Oh, I don't like it, then." Her mind was so set on not liking this artist that even though she initially enjoyed the song, she immediately convinced herself otherwise.

After reading Michelle Obama's memoir, *Becoming*, I publicly shared an inspirational quote that was not political in any way, yet it sparked some seriously nasty pushback. Had I not credited the source, those same people would have probably appreciated the quote.

This didn't simply happen because I quoted the wife of a former president. Even when I quote Gandhi, a few people always bring up how terribly he treated his wife. And when I'm brave enough to quote Mother Teresa, watch out! There's a wave of detailed accounts listing all the horrible things in which she was allegedly involved.

These incidents shed light on an interesting human tendency: we ignore fantastic advice if it comes from a source we don't like, yet we embrace bad advice from people we like. This surprises me because advice is advice. It's best if we overlook the person speaking, and even see beyond the words themselves to focus on their meaning.

In response to this eruption on social media, I followed up with the question, "Are you able to separate the wisdom from the source, or would you completely dismiss advice depending on its origin?" Many people said they gauge the worthiness of a message based on the credibility of the source. This it problematic because if we are looking for a perfect messenger from whom to receive worthwhile teachings, we will never find one. To err is human, after all.

We need to stop putting people on pedestals, and we need to stop putting people down. Let's look at everyone at eye level, as equals, capable of both great insight and horrible misdeeds.

The entire concept of credibility is faulty because someone with a squeaky-clean background is capable of horrific acts, and someone with a difficult past can spend the rest of their lives doing incredible work in the world.

So, let's trust ourselves to read a quote regardless of who said it, and decide whether it applies to us or not. We don't need anyone to validate wisdom for us in order for it to have value.

"If you don't define yourself,
you will be quickly (and inaccurately)
defined by others."
—Michelle Obama

Identity Crisis

If your happiness depends on things or people you could lose, you will spend your entire life afraid of losing them. But if your happiness depends on **who you are**, then it is firmly rooted in something you grow and evolve but never lose.

From that seat of pure awareness, everything and everyone can come or go in and out of your life (as they naturally would anyway), yet you wouldn't live in fear. Even when you lose people, your job, health, wealth, and youth, you wouldn't feel like you've lost "everything," because the most important thing is still there: your sense of purpose.

It's imperative to answer the question "Who are you?" without describing anything temporary about yourself. We spend so much time sculpting the outward expression of who we are, but if those things were taken from us (family members, photographs, records of educational achievements, your credit score, citizenship, home, and even your name), what would be left?

THAT is who you are. That's your essence.

So, let's get to know WHO we are instead of WHAT we are.

Every single life experience is an opportunity for us to define who we are in relation to what is happening. Not to judge it as "good" or "bad," but to decide, in that moment, how we want to show up.

Who am I? Well, I am not what has happened in my life, nor anything I've done, I am who I choose to become today. As difficult as it may be to leave identities behind, it's much more difficult to continue carrying them after they no longer serve their purpose (or even work against us).

An identity crisis is when we find ourselves no longer fitting into an old mold. This can be problematic if we identity as young and healthy, for example, or as single, married, or anything else that's fluid (gender identity, sexual identity, and political identity are all perfect examples of this).

A similar internal conflict occurs in many Christians when their churches aren't Christlike. For the rest of us, who we truly are sometimes clashes with who we thought we were, and other times, our behavior clashes with who we wish to be.

The solution is for us to be at peace with ourselves without any labels. We can accept each moment as an invitation to present our true selves. Life is a moment-by-moment invitation for each of us to answer the question: Who do you want to be in relation to what is happening regardless of who others expect you to be?

When you act from the deepest core of your being, you might just see who you really are... perhaps for the first time. And you would never again live in fear of losing anything because nobody can take you away from you.

So, who are you?

Don't tell me. Show me.

"Actions don't only speak louder than words,
they speak more honestly."

Money

I look at time the way most people look at money: we can waste it, spend it, or invest it. So when someone actually asked me what I spend my money on, I instinctively told him, "I don't spend time or money, I invest!"

That simple switch in perspective has significantly and directly impacted my lifestyle very deeply. When we start looking at our expenses in terms of us investing rather than spending money, we introduce a deep breath between our impulse to buy something and actually buying it.

When we breathe deeply between our impulse to buy something and actually buying it, we have time to calculate whether something is worth its price or if we are simply throwing money at a problem. Take what's called a "Convenience Fee," for example (when you purchase something like theater tickets online instead of at the theater). This so-called "Convenience Fee" counts on you taking what initially appears to be an easy way out, but if it buries you deeper into debt (if you are already in it), it's not so convenient, is it?

When you spend money you don't have, you are stealing from yourself.

I can't imagine paying someone to cut my hair, for example; I can do it myself for free. My food budget, however, may seem insanely high in the eyes of another. There isn't a single rule that applies to everyone. We each decide the value of something and how much we think it is worth. There is no "right" or "wrong" answer. To find YOUR answer, simply ask yourself if you are spending money or investing money. Are you comfortable with your answer? We all make our own choices, and we all pay our own prices.

I regularly go kayaking around the marina, and a friend recently asked me if it's difficult to live my simple life when I'm surrounded by other people's expensive homes, yachts, and jet skis? I think it's actually easier because when I see those mansions, sports cars, and Apple watches, I also see the 40-80 hour work week, the stress, the ulcers, and the headaches, and I want none of it.

My friend Dwayne says, "Drunk people made me stop drinking, and church people made me stop going to church." I guess rich people made me stop chasing money.

I don't recommend you live on the streets like I used to in order to appreciate how far you can stretch a dollar. I just think it's important to acknowledge how far a single dollar can go.

"Money can't buy
love,
happiness,
inner-peace,
integrity,
character,
manners,
respect,
morals,
trust,
patience,
or common sense.

Money can buy a house,
but not a home.
Money can buy a clock,
but not time.
Money can buy knowledge,
but not wisdom."

Focus

Focus is similar to the law of reverse effort (if you try to stay on the surface of water you sink, but when you try to sink, you float). What you think about you bring about, but if you focus too much on one thing, you miss out on something else. Sometimes we do it by choice (like when you focus on work to keep your mind off something more personal or painful), but most of the time, we have no idea that we are focused on the wrong thing.

When we imagine the life we want, we tend to focus on what we think will get us there rather than focusing on WHY we want it in the first place. Like the woman who created a vision board with a copy of her checkbook ledger on which she wrote a two million dollars deposit to manifest it into her bank account, and crazily enough, she actually got it! Thing is, the money came from a settlement agreement after she got hit by a bus while crossing the street.

You see, money was the wrong focal point all along. Instead of focusing on the life she wanted (which she thought money would make possible), she hyper-focused on the dollar amount. That's how and why we regularly miss the forest for the trees.

It's like going to the grocery store and thinking, "Don't forget the milk, don't forget the milk, don't forget the milk..." and you get home with everything but the milk because you focused on forgetting it.

We think a vacation to Hawaii will relieve our stress, but trust me, I've seen many tourists on the islands stressing about the most trivial things. If we can lose sight of the fact that we are in paradise while we are actually in it, then the old saying "Changing your perspective can change your life" really starts to make sense.

Even in relationships, the 80/20 rule dictates that the most you can reasonably expect is to have 80% of your needs met by your partner, but if someone new offers you the 20% that you don't get at home, you don't leave the 80 for the 20!

There are many examples of how big a role our focus plays in our lives, yet we rarely pause to question or adjust it.

Many years ago, when I decided to quit my corporate job and simplify my life, the law firm tried to get me to stay by offering to double my salary and lighten my workload.

I didn't know what I wanted to do with my life, but I knew for sure that a corporate job in a cubicle under fluorescent lights was not it, so no amount of money was going to incentivize me to stay.

Having a strong resolve is how we resist the temptations to veer off our chosen path.

So, as you set your life intentions, pause for a moment to focus on WHY you want the things you do... What's the reason behind it? What are you really after?

When we know the answer to **those** questions, we actually grow to crave what's good for us, and anything that distracts us from it becomes unappealing.

If it's happiness you want, just remember that happy people focus on what they have, while unhappy people focus on what's missing.

Where's your focus?

"When you focus on problems,
you get more problems.
When you focus on possibilities,
you get more opportunities."

Fluidity

I recently asked a 90-year-old woman if after everything she has witnessed in her life (from social integration to border protection, gender fluidity, orientation flexibility, diseases, cures, depressions, recessions, and so on), does she feel hopeful or woeful?

She told me that because social change tends to come in waves (often swinging from one extreme to the next), she doesn't worry about things like walls going up, for example, because she has seen them eventually come down.

She is also not concerned about the never-ending wars between nations or the rich and the poor, nor is she bothered by the endless turmoil between religious extremists and the reformed, or the seemingly simple yet constantly difficult line to draw between Church and State, because those things, she said, "Go around and round in circles."

The only thing she **is** pessimistic about is the environment because it's the one thing she hasn't seen go from bad to good, back to bad and good again. "It just keeps getting worse in a downward spiral."

I asked her what she thinks of the young generation today wanting to blame her generation for destroying the planet. She laughed and said, "It's true we didn't recycle newspapers to make paper towels, but we used cloth napkins and returned milk, soda, and beer bottles to be sterilized and refilled. We didn't have reusable grocery bags, but we used the brown paper bags from the market as trash bags at home or to cover our schoolbooks."

She said her mom used the fabric from old clothes to make dresses for her dolls, saving the buttons and zippers to be used later on. "We washed and reused baby diapers because we didn't have the throw-away kind," she said. "We dried our clothes on the line, harnessing wind and solar power long before Elon Musk was around."

Now, she volunteers at the local thrift store, where she said she regularly sees perfectly good household items tossed aside like trash because someone replaced them with something new.

"I'm from a time when if something was broken, we would fix it, not throw it away," she said. "I don't know what else I can do to save the planet, except continue telling people to stop having children."

We both chuckled at that, even though everything we discussed was rather heavy.

Surprisingly, I did not feel doomed when we ended our conversation. It's quite possible that even the big environmental changes we worry about occur every few thousand years, so we can't witness those changes within one lifetime the way we experience social change.

I don't have any answers, and neither did she. But I'm not scared, even if the destiny for most of us is to be wiped out in one way or another just to start again as fellow survivors of a planet that reboots itself every billion years. I don't know what will happen, but I know that we don't need to wait for our planet to become inhabitable to start treating it more gently. We can start doing that right now.

Your behavior is what matters. What you do matters. And, therefore, you matter!

Let's all be as cool, calm, peaceful, and collected as this 90-year-old lady can be regardless of what's going on in the world. She holds it all so lightly; there didn't seem to be a tight, rigid grip on anything because she sees it all as fluid.

"You can only lose what you cling to."

Wabi-Sabi

I used to think that striving to be a perfectionist was a positive personality trait. It meant attention to detail, hard work, and diligently aiming for what is best without settling for less. But what is perfection? And... according to whom? Perfection implies a hierarchy and judgment of "better" or "worse," comparing everything to some ideal or standard to which we are all subjected.

Our obsession with perfection starts with getting perfect grades, having the perfect body, perfectly rounded or sharp corners, perfect teeth, or a perfect score. We thrive on terms like "excellence," "proper," and "appropriate," and we are drawn to symmetry and balance. I didn't even realize I was judging the world this way until I heard the Japanese term Wabi-Sabi, which actually celebrates asymmetry, rough edges, the incomplete, the simple, and the natural integrity and impermanence of everything as it is.

After many years of me trying to measure up to one idea of perfection, Wabi-Sabi is a refreshing practice that embraces what is slightly marred, scarred, aged, nature-made, and jagged. I'm not just talking about aesthetics; the more I think about my old definition of perfection, the more I realize how I've been measuring everything and everyone against impossible standards. Wabi-Sabi doesn't lower the standard, it changes it.

There is no English word for Wabi-Sabi. The closest words I can think of are "rustic" or "makeshift," neither of which capture the magic of it all.

Years ago, when I took a ceramics class, the cereal bowl I made wasn't perfectly round, so I threw it away. I completely overlooked the fact that my bowl's uniqueness was not only what gave it value, it would have served its purpose just fine (had I kept it).

Wabi-Sabi has helped me shift from looking at something to determine if it's perfect, efficient, or ideal, to simply asking "Does it work?" Never mind if it's a little wobbly, slightly uneven or off-center... If it works, it's perfect. Wabi-Sabi is an invitation to ease up, loosen our grip, and forget the conventional idea of perfection.

While traveling in a third-world country, I witnessed Wabi-Sabi embodied in various ways: a guy on a motorcycle with a broken headlight using a flashlight, farmers spreading unhusked rice grains onto the hot pavement to dry in the sun, mismatched utensils, hand-drawn street signs, and huts built entirely out of old plastic bottles. Everyone was a modern-day MacGyver out of necessity, and it not only worked, it's perfect!

I hope the concept of Wabi-Sabi offers you as great a relief from the burden of judgment as it has given me. This may either be a tiny shift for you or a massive undertaking, but either way, let's practice Wabi-Sabi to redefine perfection!

> "Our search for perfection
> causes suffering."

Abundance

Saying, "I just want things to go back to the way they used to be" is a common but impossible wish because everything is constantly changing. Circumstances can improve or get worse, but they can never go back to the way they were.

When I have tried to move on from a traumatic incident, a painful breakup, or a great loss, it took me a long time to heal because I kept trying to return to the person I was before the hurt, but that person was long gone. It was only after I began breathing life into a new me that I started developing into the person I am today.

When we hit a snag in relationships, we try to get the relationship back to the way it was before the bump in the road. But each experience changes us, so we can't recreate yesterday's outcome with today's ingredients. Real growth can only come when we embrace the newness of one another and stop focusing on the past.

I used to be a lot of things, but none of them define me. For example, after playing a lot of volleyball in my 20s, I took a break for a couple of decades and then decided to play again in my 40s. I was disappointed that I couldn't jump as high anymore. Instead of having fun on the court without comparing myself to how I used to be, I made the mistake of trying to keep up with the younger players, and I ended up with a bruised ego and a busted knee.

We can never be who we once were, which is great news IF we celebrate and focus on who we are becoming in this moment.

So, when it comes to our health, wealth, and youth, let's not compare today with yesterday, but rather focus on the abundance in our lives right now.

In other words, stop looking back; you're not going that way!

Ill-Will

There are five challenges to staying on the path of mindfulness: desire, laziness, a scattered mind, doubt, and ill-will. The feeling of ill will toward others (wishing for something unpleasant to happen to someone else) stems from something unpleasant within us.

I recently met someone who was so rude, greedy, selfish, and hateful, I can only imagine how miserable she must be. In her desperate attempt to feel good, superior, important, or powerful, she apparently needs to view others as inferior and unworthy.

She consciously made a decision that negatively impacted others but benefited her, and I admit to feeling the ill-will impulse to be vindictive and hurtful right back. But, when I started looking at my own desire to hurt her, I remembered that "hurt people hurt people." My desire to hurt her stemmed from my own disappointment, as if causing pain to someone else would somehow relieve me of my own. So, instead of trying to find ways to make her life worse, I figured she must already be suffering enough or she wouldn't be treating people the way she does.

Thoughts become words, and words become actions. If I were a Zen master, maybe I could control my thoughts, but I am not. So, I do the next best thing: I use mindfulness to control my words and actions, which is a good place to start.

I hope we can all lengthen the pause between impulse and response, and treat everyone with kindness, patience, and generosity. Feel the ill-will, explore it, release it, and then go sit next to Rumi.

"Beyond 'Right' and 'Wrong' there is a field,
I will meet you there."
— Rumi

Equanimity

I've been taught that we create our own stress whenever we want to be anywhere other than where we are. If it's cold outside, we wish it were warmer, and when it's hot, we want it to be cooler. My uncle used to say, "I just want one dollar more than I have," which perfectly illustrates the endlessness of this vicious cycle.

At one point, we probably dreamed of being where we are today, and now that we're here, we wish to be somewhere else (if not physically, then in our spiritual evolution, relationships, careers, etc.).

It makes me wonder if we are robbing ourselves of contentment by chasing happiness.

I think the only way to combat this conundrum is to learn to crave what we already have (not just accept or appreciate it, but actually long for what **is** instead of dreaming of what was or is yet to be).

It's impossible to be content if we are always comparing everything to how much better we imagine it could be. There has got to be a point of exhalation, acceptance, and peace, where instead of chasing happiness, we bask in the glorious blissfulness of contentment.

If our source of happiness is rooted in what the Buddha called Worldly Concerns (such as seeking sense pleasures and avoiding unpleasant sensations, attachment to wealth and praise, or aversion to loss and blame), we may gain temporary happiness from time to time, but it will be accompanied by fear, restlessness, and concern, all of which make us miserable.

Even if our happiness comes from achieving temporary peace of mind, we would still be at risk of losing it to greed, hatred, and ignorance. So, let's consider a different definition of happiness; something less dependent on unstable, fleeting, fragile, and unpredictable circumstances, and more closely related to equanimity, which is not associated with the absence of challenges, it's the ability to remain calm and serene despite adversity.

Equanimity is synonymous with composure, which is a state of being balanced, collected, and in control of yourself. So, whenever I lose my cool (it happens), I immediately check to see if I accidentally stepped in one of those Worldly Concerns (such as attachment or aversion), and without fail (every time), it turns out that I have. So, I scrape it off, acknowledge where I veered off my intended path of equanimity, and regain composure.

This doesn't mean I don't care about what goes on in the world (equanimity is not insensitivity nor apathy); it means my efforts to make the world a better place remain undisturbed by complications, disappointments, and setbacks.

Think of it like working diligently to pay off debt while monthly bills and unexpected expenses slow us down. Equanimity means making peace with the fact that the debt will always be there, but we continue making payments without losing sight of the progress already made. Little by little, we get closer to a state in which nothing that arises (internally or externally) makes us agitated. Equanimity is sustainable and dependent solely on our mind's ability to return to the middle path where nothing and no-one can disturb it.

Now, doesn't that sound like a very happy life (by the new definition of the word)?

Pretend you are given one life to live; would you spend it pursuing happiness the way you have been, or would you aim for equanimity?

The amount of work is the same, but the experience will be completely different.

> "Even a happy life cannot be without a measure of darkness.
> It is far better to take things as they come
> with patience and equanimity."
> — Carl Jung

The End

The intention behind each story in this book is for us to contemplate certain topics and perhaps even discuss them more openly when social etiquette considers them uncomfortable or taboo.

We have tackled insecurities, judgment, identity, and forgiveness, among many other subjects, and now, as the book is coming to an end, I figured we could talk about "the end."

Regardless of race, gender, religion, age, political affiliation, or even species classification, the one thing we all have in common is the very thing we've been raised not to discuss or think about: death. Any mention of death is often considered morbid, defined by the dictionary as "an abnormal and unhealthy interest in disturbing and unpleasant subjects."

Death is not the opposite of life; it's part of it. We can't avoid the pain it causes by refusing to talk about it.

Isn't that exactly what the Buddha's father tried to do? He sheltered his young son from any mention of old age, sickness, and death. Our culture celebrates youth and vitality by efficiently filing the elderly and less-abled into retirement communities, practically out of sight. How are we supposed to develop a healthy relationship with these facts of life and death if we don't see or talk about them on a regular basis?

The rule of thumb that we've discussed is that visibility leads to acceptance (the more often we encounter something, the more comfortable we become with its existence). This is true about interracial couples, women in power, same-gender couples, blue hair, and so on. Conversely, the less often we see something, the less prepared we are to deal with it.

Even if you have seen a corpse, it was probably in a coffin, wearing makeup, and dressed in fine apparel. This gives a whole new meaning to "out of sight, out of mind." If we don't see it, then we don't have to deal with it, which isn't the case.

Whether it's our own death or the death of a loved one, we all have to deal with it. If we are not prepared for death in whatever form it comes, then the experience can be downright devastating when it doesn't have to be.

How is it that death is all around us, but we are still shocked by it? From a very young age, life has prepared us for death's inevitability. As kids, most of us have experienced the loss of a goldfish or a dog, for example, or perhaps even grandparents, parents, or friends, often without any warning, and sometimes very early on. Yet people still claim to be devastated by the loss of a loved one who was taken "unexpectedly." How is that possible?

Even if they mean the timing was unexpected, having an expectation that someone (anyone) would live to be a certain age before they die is proof that we are not honest with ourselves about death's seemingly irrational timing.

Somehow, in our generally overly pessimistic society, we are unreasonably optimistic about how long everyone we know is going to live, including ourselves.

Let's be more honest with ourselves and with our children about the fact that anyone's last breath could happen at any moment. I think it would help us appreciate each other and life itself a whole lot more. We would save ourselves much devastation while learning to celebrate every living moment, don't you think?

May this be the end (of living mindlessly).

"Even death is not to be feared
by one who has lived wisely."
— The Buddha

Also by Timber Hawkeye

BUDDHIST BOOT CAMP

When I left the corporate world and moved to Hawaii, I started emailing my friends and family a short letter each month to let them know what's going on in my life. About eight years later, my friend Kim suggested that I share those emails on a blog (simply because she found the letters inspirational, and she figured other people would benefit from reading them as well). As it turns out, Kim was right! The blog became a book, and many people found the simple message in those chapters refreshing, inspirational, and empowering. The book is available in multiple languages; it is used as part of the required-reading curriculum in a few schools; it is available in paperback at prison libraries all over the world; it has been part of many book clubs and discussion circles; and of course, it sparked the Buddhist Boot Camp Podcast, on which The Opposite of Namaste was based.

FAITHFULLY RELIGIONLESS
A Memoir About Letting Go of the Need to Know

If you and I were to go on a hike, and you were to ask me for my life story, that's what Faithfully Religionless explores.

In fact, if you get the audiobook, it will sound like I'm right next to you, telling you all about my journey of discovering the difference between feelings and emotions, the disparity between truths and facts, and the countless benefits of mindful living.

For more information, please visit TimberHawkeye.com

CPSIA information can be obtained
at www.ICGtesting.com
Printed in the USA
BVHW041147230223
659075BV00001B/28

9 781946 005830